# WILLIAM FAULKNER

OTHER TITLES IN THE GREENHAVEN PRESS
LITERARY COMPANION SERIES:

## AMERICAN AUTHORS

Maya Angelou
Stephen Crane
Emily Dickinson
F. Scott Fitzgerald
Nathaniel Hawthorne
Ernest Hemingway
Herman Melville
Arthur Miller
Eugene O'Neill
Edgar Allan Poe
John Steinbeck
Mark Twain

## BRITISH AUTHORS

Jane Austen
Joseph Conrad
Charles Dickens

## WORLD AUTHORS

Fyodor Dostoyevsky
Homer
Sophocles

## AMERICAN LITERATURE

The Great Gatsby
Of Mice and Men
The Scarlet Letter

## BRITISH LITERATURE

Animal Farm
The Canterbury Tales
Lord of the Flies
Romeo and Juliet
Shakespeare: The Comedies
Shakespeare: The Sonnets
Shakespeare: The Tragedies
A Tale of Two Cities

## WORLD LITERATURE

Diary of a Young Girl

THE GREENHAVEN PRESS
*Literary Companion*
TO AMERICAN AUTHORS

READINGS ON

# WILLIAM FAULKNER

David Bender, *Publisher*
Bruno Leone, *Executive Editor*
Brenda Stalcup, *Managing Editor*
Bonnie Szumski, *Series Editor*
Clarice Swisher, *Book Editor*

Greenhaven Press, San Diego, CA

Library of Congress Cataloging-in-Publication Data

Readings on William Faulkner / Clarice Swisher, book editor.
        p.       cm. — (The Greenhaven Press literary
    companion to American authors)
        Includes bibliographical references and index.
        ISBN 1-56510 641 5 (lib. : alk. paper). —
    ISBN 1-56510-640-7 (pbk. : alk. paper)
        1. Faulkner, William, 1897–1962—Criticism and
    interpretation. 2. Mississippi—In literature. I. Swisher,
    Clarice, 1933–   . II. Series.
    PS3511.A8694694    1998
    813'.52—dc21                                    97-12900
                                                        CIP

Cover photo: UPI/Bettmann

Copyright ©1998 by Greenhaven Press, Inc.
PO Box 289009
San Diego, CA 92198-9009
Printed in the U.S.A.

**"The poet's voice need not merely be the record of man; it can be one of the props, the pillars to help him endure and prevail."**

—*William Faulkner*
*Nobel Acceptance Speech, 1950*

# CONTENTS

## Chapter 1: Major Themes and Techniques in Faulkner's Works

### 1. Faulkner's Portrayal of the South
*by Michael Millgate*                                       32

William Faulkner selects vivid imagery from the South, his home nearly all his life, to invent the fictional Yoknapatawpha County, the setting for his novels. He uses representative characters and events to portray universal emotions and themes.

### 2. Faulkner's Novels Are Experimental
*by Maxwell Geismar*                                        39

Experimenting with new forms of internal dialogue, William Faulkner both depicts the despair of isolated individuals and criticizes the society in which they live. In a broader context, Faulkner portrays the end of an agricultural way of life in the South and the rise of commercialism.

### 3. Humor in Faulkner's Works
*by Harry Modean Campbell and Ruel E. Foster*              43

Faulkner uses two kinds of humor, surrealistic and frontier, to give a bitter, sardonic tone to a situation or to soften the shock of violent or antisocial behavior.

### 4. Faulkner's Use of Motion as Metaphor
*by Richard P. Adams*                                       54

Throughout his works, William Faulkner seeks to freeze motion—of events, thought processes, aging—because continual change makes accurate description impossible.

## Chapter 2: Faulkner's Most Anthologized Stories

### 1. Atmosphere and Theme in "A Rose for Emily"
*by Ray B. West Jr.*                                        65

In "A Rose for Emily," William Faulkner contrasts elements from the past and present to create a distorted, unreal atmosphere.

# Chapter 3: Faulkner's Major Works: 1929–1932

of her child, remains optimistic despite her troubles, while Joe Christmas and Gail Hightower struggle with mistakes and agonies of the past. Hightower connects the stories and unifies the book.

## Chapter 4: Major Works After 1932

# FOREWORD

*"'Tis the good reader that
makes the good book."*

Ralph Waldo Emerson

The story's bare facts are simple: The captain, an old and scarred seafarer, walks with a peg leg made of whale ivory. He relentlessly drives his crew to hunt the world's oceans for the great white whale that crippled him. After a long search, the ship encounters the whale and a fierce battle ensues. Finally the captain drives his harpoon into the whale, but the harpoon line catches the captain about the neck and drags him to his death.

A simple story, a straightforward plot—yet, since the 1851 publication of Herman Melville's *Moby-Dick*, readers and critics have found many meanings in the struggle between Captain Ahab and the whale. To some, the novel is a cautionary tale that depicts how Ahab's obsession with revenge leads to his insanity and death. Others believe that the whale represents the unknowable secrets of the universe and that Ahab is a tragic hero who dares to challenge fate by attempting to discover this knowledge. Perhaps Melville intended Ahab as a criticism of Americans' tendency to become involved in well-intentioned but irrational causes. Or did Melville model Ahab after himself, letting his fictional character express his anger at what he perceived as a cruel and distant god?

Although literary critics disagree over the meaning of *Moby-Dick*, readers do not need to choose one particular interpretation in order to gain an understanding of Melville's novel. Instead, by examining various analyses, they can gain numerous insights into the issues that lie under the surface of the basic plot. Studying the writings of literary critics can also aid readers in making their own assessments of *Moby-Dick* and other literary works and in developing analytical thinking skills.

The Greenhaven Literary Companion Series was created with these goals in mind. Designed for young adults, this unique anthology series provides an engaging and comprehensive introduction to literary analysis and criticism. The essays included in the Literary Companion Series are chosen for their accessibility to a young adult audience and are expertly edited in consideration of both the reading and comprehension levels of this audience. In addition, each essay is introduced by a concise summation that presents the contributing writer's main themes and insights. Every anthology in the Literary Companion Series contains a varied selection of critical essays that cover a wide time span and express diverse views. Wherever possible, primary sources are represented through excerpts from authors' notebooks, letters, and journals and through contemporary criticism.

Each title in the Literary Companion Series pays careful consideration to the historical context of the particular author or literary work. In-depth biographies and detailed chronologies reveal important aspects of authors' lives and emphasize the historical events and social milieu that influenced their writings. To facilitate further research, every anthology includes primary and secondary source bibliographies of articles and/or books selected for their suitability for young adults. These engaging features make the Greenhaven Literary Companion Series ideal for introducing students to literary analysis in the classroom or as a library resource for young adults researching the world's great authors and literature.

Exceptional in its focus on young adults, the Greenhaven Literary Companion Series strives to present literary criticism in a compelling and accessible format. Every title in the series is intended to spark readers' interest in leading American and world authors, to help them broaden their understanding of literature, and to encourage them to formulate their own analyses of the literary works that they read. It is the editors' hope that young adult readers will find these anthologies to be true companions in their study of literature.

# INTRODUCTION

When William Faulkner accepted the Nobel Prize for literature in 1950, many people considered Faulkner's great theme to be human decline and despair; characters in his stories and novels, after all, frequently experience hardship, suffering, poverty, isolation, cruelty, indifference, and stupidity. The audience assembled for the Nobel celebrations was surprised at the uplifting urgency of the words in his acceptance speech:

> It is easy enough to say that man is immortal simply because he will endure; that when the last ding-dong of doom has clanged and faded from the last worthless rock hanging tideless in the last red and dying evening, that even then there will still be one more sound: that of his puny inexhaustible voice, still talking. I refuse to accept this. I believe that man will not merely endure: he will prevail. He is immortal, not because he alone among creatures has an inexhaustible voice, but because he has a soul, a spirit capable of compassion and sacrifice and endurance.

Believing that the human soul is worth "the agony and the sweat" that writing requires, Faulkner dedicated the recognition of his prize to the young writer. He advised him or her never to be afraid and always to write about

> the old verities and truths of the heart, the old universal truths lacking which any story is ephemeral and doomed— love and honor and pity and pride and compassion and sacrifice. Until he does so he labors under a curse. He writes not of love but of lust, of defeats in which nobody loses anything of value, of victories without hope and worst of all without pity and compassion. His griefs grieve on no universal bones, leaving no scars. He writes not of the heart but of the glands.

Critics had misread and misunderstood Faulkner's work perhaps because he wrote not in a linear or logical order, but in an experimental stream-of-consciousness style; that is, Faulkner records what flows in the minds of his characters—observations of action and dialogue, memories, feelings, thoughts—in the order, the stream, of consciousness.

The style is supposed to imitate real consciousness and reveal the inner nature of a character.

Critic Malcolm Cowley did much to make Faulkner's works better known and better understood. In his essays he explained Faulkner's attempt to create a mythical county in northern Mississippi and the characters who populate it.

Today, Faulkner is still read by many people and his works are considered classic. *Readings on William Faulkner* assembles a collection of American and British critics who help students discover how to read Faulkner's prose and find glimpses into the "soul capable of compassion and sacrifice and endurance." Some of the contributors explain techniques that Faulkner employed in numerous works, such as internal dialogue, characters in counterpoint, and shifting points of view. Other critics alert students to recurring themes in the stories and novels, such as nature, racial oppression, and the decay of the past.

*Readings on William Faulkner* includes many special features that make research and literary criticism accessible and understandable. An annotated table of contents lets readers quickly preview the contents of individual essays. A chronology features a list of significant events in Faulkner's life placed in a broader historical context. The bibliography includes books on Faulkner's time and additional critical sources suitable for further research.

Each essay has aids for clear understanding. The introductions serve as directed reading for the essays by explaining the main points, which are then identified by subheads within the essays. Footnotes identify uncommon references and define unfamiliar words. Inserts, many taken from Faulkner's novels, illustrate points made in the essays and the power of Faulkner's prose. Taken together, these aids make Greenhaven Press's Literary Companion Series an indispensable research tool.

# WILLIAM FAULKNER: A BIOGRAPHY

William Faulkner was two years old at the dawn of the twentieth century, a century of dramatic international crises and social upheaval that affected Faulkner's personal life. During his lifetime, America witnessed World War I, the stock market crash, the depression, World War II, the Korean War, the civil rights movement, and the election of John F. Kennedy to the presidency. In Faulkner's South, still smarting from the Civil War, the old aristocracy lost control of powerful institutions and gave way to a rising commercial middle class. In his personal life, Faulkner overcame the public's opinion that he acted like an aristocrat who amounted to nothing and the nickname "Count No Count" to win the Nobel Prize for literature and to achieve worldwide acclaim as a novelist.

William Cuthbert Faulkner, called Billy as a child, was born on September 25, 1897, in New Albany, Mississippi. The first of four children born to Maud and Murry Falkner, Billy had three younger brothers: Jack, Johncy, and Dean. Billy's maternal grandmother, Lelia Butler, whom Faulkner called Damuddy, enjoyed drawing and painting. His mother, Maud Falkner, a graduate of Women's College in Columbia, Mississippi, enjoyed reading Shakespeare, Conrad, Tennyson, and Browning. For four generations, the Falkners, as the name was originally spelled, held prominent positions in law, farming, real estate, politics, and business and were well known throughout Mississippi. Murry Falkner attended the University of Mississippi for two years, then worked as an administrator of his grandfather's railroad until it was sold and his family helped him start another business. The Falkner family was a close clan, confident of their place and their leadership, a part of the prosperous old southern aristocracy.

## FAULKNER'S CHILDHOOD

Billy's childhood was ordinary in most ways; his family offered love and support, and experienced success and conflict not unlike that of most families. As the firstborn, Faulkner formed a close relationship with his mother that he maintained until her death. His second "mother" was the black family servant, Caroline Barr, whom the boys called Mammy Callie; she loved and disciplined the Falkner boys and told them thrilling stories of her people and the slave days of her ancestors. After the Old Colonel (Faulkner's great-grandfather) sold the railroad in 1902, Murry moved his family to Oxford, Mississippi, the seat of Lafayette County, a town with a population of eighteen hundred. Billy excelled as a student in the Oxford elementary school, which he entered in 1905 as a first grader, skipping kindergarten and, later, second grade. He worked hard at reading, spelling, writing, and arithmetic and earned perfect or excellent marks in all those subjects, but he most liked to draw and tell stories. He became as good a storyteller as Mammy Callie and knew as a boy that he wanted to be a writer. He played ordinary tricks on his younger brothers, and he entertained them with his imaginative games. Biographer Joseph Blotner reports an anecdote in which Billy, whose chore was to haul in wood, persuaded a friend to do the hauling in exchange for stories. He kept his friend working all winter by leaving a story just before the climax, promising to finish it the next day.

Faulkner was influenced by both parents. A subtle family tension generated by the personality differences between his parents caused conflicting expectations for Faulkner. Murry Falkner typified a certain machismo in the Falkner clan; he had fought a duel in his youth, he drank hard liquor, and he hunted with men who elaborated on their hunting exploits. Faulkner was expected to carry on the strongly masculine family tradition, while Maud wanted her sons to be educated for gentler roles and to read classical literature. Murry, who had loved the railroad and regretted its sale, sought solace in the stables of his new livery business, where he tended the horses, read western novels, and dreamed of cattle ranching. He showed a dark, cold, aloof side, especially in the presence of his wife. Maud tried to be stoic about his attitude; a sign in her kitchen read "Don't complain, don't explain." Tension notwithstanding, there were pleasant family outings, rides in the country, and elaborate holiday celebrations; Billy went fishing with his dad and riding in the surrey with his grandfather. Many times during their marriage, however, Maud took her husband to treatment when he had been drinking too much. Traits of both parents eventually manifested themselves in their eldest son—his mother's love of literature and art and his father's strong, aloof manner and, unfortunately, alcoholism.

## FAULKNER'S TEEN YEARS

Faulkner became bored with school in sixth grade and often rebelled against standard course requirements. He drew pictures and wrote stories during lessons and skipped classes to go to his uncle's or grandfather's libraries to read medical and law books. In seventh grade, in place of the regular curriculum, Faulkner read *Moby Dick* (though his mother insisted he do his homework). His deskmate, Ralph Muckenfuss, thought Billy "the laziest boy I ever saw." In English, he answered the simplest questions with "I don't know." By high school, many students thought he was strange and called him "quair"; in eleventh grade, he attended school just to play sports and never went back to graduate. He felt socially inferior for not being a successful Falkner leader, but he also felt intellectually superior and longed to pursue private interests, a conflict he lived with for many years. Faulkner's alienation from school parallels his alienation from his family. He grew distant from his mother and hostile toward his father; he was withdrawn from his brothers and silent with everyone in his family. Fortunately, he found close relationships outside his family.

He developed an important relationship with his first girlfriend, Estelle Oldham. The two of them enjoyed many hours together: Estelle played the piano and Billy listened, they read and discussed the poetry of A.E. Housman, Shakespeare, and Keats, and Billy wrote nature and romantic verses for her. Billy fell in love with her, but there were obstacles; she was two years older and popular with boys in school, and her family expected her to marry a successful young man from a wealthy family. Estelle played the dutiful daughter and married Cornell Franklin in 1918, as her family wished her to do.

Faulkner's friendships with Phil Stone and Ben Wasson guided his education and supported his writing career. Phil Stone, who was four years older, a graduate of the University of Mississippi and a Yale law student, loved literature and became Faulkner's mentor. He gave Faulkner books, especially the works of classical Greek writers and contemporary poets, whose form and ideas they discussed together. Stone invited Faulkner to join his family at their hunting camp where Stone initiated Faulkner into the traditional rituals of food, drink, storytelling, and the etiquette of hunting. Faulkner later used the experience while writing "The Bear."

## FAULKNER'S TWENTIES

When the United States entered World War I, Faulkner wanted to do his patriotic duty and enlist in the air force, but he was rejected as too short—he was five feet, five inches tall—and too light. Humiliated, he went to Canada and joined the Royal Air Force by convincing recruiters that he was British. After 179 days of basic training, however, the war ended, and Private Faulkner was honorably discharged without ever flying or seeing combat. For years, he fabricated a military career. He purchased an RAF uniform, which he wore home to Mississippi, and told stories about his heroic exploits and the wounds he received during his RAF service.

Faulkner's restlessness prompted many trips, mostly in the South, storing up material he used in his writing and making valuable acquaintances. Often he went to New Orleans, where he attended parties and tried various manners and styles as he searched for his identity. Through Phil Stone, Faulkner met Stark Young, a teacher at Amherst College who felt the young writer had talent but was doing little to develop or use it. Young invited Faulkner to New York, got him a job at a Doubleday bookstore, and directed him in studies of Melville, Conrad, Balzac, Flaubert, Dickens, Dostoyevsky, Cervantes, and literary criticism. Young said of Faulkner, "He succeeded in educating himself more thoroughly, and in some ways more systematically, than most graduate students are educated." Restless again, Faulkner hopped a steamer to Europe and went to the Montparnasse district of Paris, where he mingled with intellectuals and artists. He was especially influenced by impressionist painting, an artistic style he was later able to express as prose. Like the impressionist artists, Faulkner created images that conveyed the emotional truth of people and places, rather than depicting their physical likenesses.

Oxford was his home base; to Oxford he returned from travels to earn money and redirect his life. Relatives helped him land jobs, but he failed at all of them. Hired at his grand-father's bank in Oxford, he did no work and was let go. He did odd jobs painting and cleaning, but quit to travel again. He got tired of his New York bookstore job, neglected the customers, and was fired. For a time, he was a Boy Scout leader, but was dismissed for drinking. When a relative used influence to make him postmaster of the University of Mississippi campus post office, he turned the back room into a reading room where he and his friends read and played bridge while the customers waited. He was fired when customers complained that Faulkner held their magazines to read himself.

Faulkner was no more successful as a college student than he was as an employee. In 1919 Bill attended classes and studied French at the University of Mississippi, where his brother John was a prelaw student. On campus, he neither participated in discussions nor took exams and displayed a manner his fellow students thought arrogant. He drew cartoons for the college magazine and wrote poems for the college newspaper. He enrolled in a math class thinking it would teach him discipline, but he stopped going and dropped out. He acquired the reputation of a fool; students mocked him mercilessly in school publications and called him "Count No Count," a name that spread throughout the community. He withdrew from the University of Mississippi for good on November 5, 1920.

## FAULKNER'S WRITING CAREER BEGINS

Though he floundered academically and in business, Faulkner's writing career gradually developed. In 1919 he wrote poetry that imitated classical Greek and Roman writers, T.S. Eliot, and Conrad Aiken. Stone helped get "A Faun's Holiday" published in the *New Republic*, for which Faulkner was paid fifteen dollars, and he won a couple of writing contests. At this time, he was regularly spelling his name "Faulkner" rather than "Falkner." In 1920 he hand-produced one copy of his poems, entitled *The Lilacs*, and wrote a play for the college players which was never produced, but he sold five copies of the script at five dollars each. He wrote an eighty-four-page volume of poems entitled *Visions in Spring* for Estelle, who periodically returned to Oxford for visits. In

1921 the New Orleans magazine *Double Dealer* published another of his poems. Around this time he began writing prose pieces as well as poems; "The Hill" combines realistic prose descriptions with the symbolic imagery of poetry. In 1922 Phil Stone paid the cost of publishing *The Marble Faun,* a volume of poems. By 1925 Faulkner had sold a series of prose sketches to the New Orleans *Times Picayune.*

After his trip to Paris, Faulkner began writing novels. He started *Mosquitoes,* set it aside, and wrote *Mayday,* which was retitled *Soldiers' Pay* when American novelist and poet Sherwood Anderson's publisher accepted it. The *New York Times* called it "experimental," his father would not even open it, and the University of Mississippi library refused the copy he offered for free. *Mosquitoes,* with a reworked plot and characters modeled on his New Orleans friends, was published in 1927. With new stories came new realizations, according to biographer Joseph Blotner, quoting Faulkner: "I discovered that my own little postage stamp of native soil [Lafayette County] was worth writing about and that I would never live long enough to exhaust it." From a discussion with Phil Stone, he concluded that the major southern issue was not race, but the rise of "rednecks" who had none of the standards and morality of the old aristocrats. Prefiguring his fictional Snopes family, he began to write with little purpose

> until I realised that to make it truly evocative it must be per-
> sonal. . . . So I got some people, some I invented, others I cre-
> ated out of tales I learned of nigger cooks and stable boys of all
> ages. . . . Created, I say, because they are composed partly from
> what they were in actual life and partly from what they should
> have been and were not: Thus I improved on God, who, dra-
> matic though He be, has no sense, no feeling for theatre.

These realizations formed the fictional method he relied on through his long literary career.

In 1927 Faulkner wrote with clearer direction than ever before. He wrote *Flags in the Dust,* with characters based on people he knew; one of them, a wild man, was modeled after his great-grandfather, the Old Colonel. Published in 1929 as *Sartoris,* it received mixed reviews. He wrote *The Sound and the Fury,* which Ben Wasson, now Faulkner's New York agent, cut by one-third. When it was published in October 1929, reviewers compared Faulkner to James Joyce and Dostoyevsky, and the Boston *Evening Transcript*'s reviewer described the novel as "Greek tragedy in north Mississippi," but sales were poor. He wrote and rewrote short stories, and he began *Sanctuary*.

## MARRIAGE AND RESPONSIBILITIES

When Estelle returned to Oxford in April 1929 with her children, Victoria, called Cho Cho, and Malcolm, she had divorced Cornell Franklin. Estelle and Faulkner were married two months later in June and spent the summer honeymooning in Pascagoula, during which time Faulkner worked on the galleys for the upcoming publication of *The Sound and the Fury*. Shortly after their marriage, Faulkner bought and renovated an old farmhouse where he and Estelle had played as children and named it Rowan Oak. With a wife and stepchildren to support, Faulkner began working the twelve-hour night shift at the university power plant where he shoveled coal, a job that gave him quiet intervals for writing.

For the next twenty years, Faulkner was constantly struggling to find enough money to pay living expenses. He tried to alleviate the problem by writing potboilers, stories he could sell to national magazines for a few hundred dollars each. "A Rose for Emily" was rejected, but the *Saturday Evening Post* bought "Red Leaves" and "Lizards in Jamshyd's Courtyard" for $750 each, enough money to wire Rowan Oak for electricity. Between January and September 1930, he sold six of the thirty-seven stories he submitted. By Christmas he had written and sold four more stories and received enough money to celebrate the holiday. Shortly after New Year of 1931, Estelle gave birth to a baby girl, but the premature infant died because no incubator was available. Faulkner grieved the loss for a year.

Between 1929 and 1932, Faulkner wrote three major novels. The carefully planned *As I Lay Dying* was completed in a few weeks: While he wrote it, he realized that not only did each book require its own design, but his novels together also needed a large design. In this book he first identified his Lafayette County as the fictional Yoknapatawpha County and his Oxford as Jefferson. His books would tell the history of his "own little postage stamp of native soil." *As I Lay Dying* was published in October 1930, again with some good reviews but poor sales. The revised *Sanctuary* was published in February 1931, bringing immediate objection to its violence and praise for the power of its writing. One reviewer said it left him limp; another called it "one of the most terrifying books I have ever read. And it is one of the most extraordinary." In that summer and fall Faulkner was described as a "genius" and a writer of "great talent," and his book was called a "great novel." In Oxford, people bought the book secretly and talked about it privately, but publicly most were angered by the embarrassing implications for their city and region. In October 1931, a book of stories entitled *These 13* was published. Faulkner had already begun work on a complex novel he called *Dark House.* One evening in August just before dinner, Estelle asked Bill, "Does it ever seem to you that the light in August is different from any other time of the year?" Faulkner got up and changed the title *Dark House* to *Light in August.* It was published in October 1932.

## TRIPS TO NEW YORK AND CALIFORNIA

Faulkner, who made numerous trips to New York, where his publishers, editors, and agents were located, fell into a pattern of activities on these trips. On his first trip, in October 1931, following a gathering of southern writers in Charlottesville, Virginia, Faulkner found himself courted by publishers who thought they saw the potential for huge sales in his future works. He wrote to Estelle, "I have been meeting people and being called on all day. And I have taken in about 300.00 since I got here. It's just like I was some strange and valuable beast." Henry Hansen of the New York *World-Telegram* wrote that

> rival publishers fought a merry battle yesterday for the favors of William Faulkner, America's most promising author.... Half a dozen publishers stormed Mr. Faulkner's door, offering as high as twenty-five percent and generous advance royalties.

He met other writers at the Hotel Algonquin, a favorite literary gathering place, and they liked him. He was entertained at lavish cocktail and dinner parties hosted by publishers. As a rural southerner unused to the attention and whirl of activities, after a few weeks he longed for his quiet Mississippi home. Subsequent trips to New York followed a similar pattern: He stayed at the Algonquin, was a guest at many parties, negotiated contracts, edited manuscripts and wrote introductions, and usually drank heavily enough to require a stay in private homes or hospitals to recover.

During his New York visits, he signed contracts with major movie producers from California, either for rights to make a movie based on one of his stories or books or for jobs to write scripts for films. For example, he signed a six-week screenwriting contract for five hundred dollars a week with Metro-Goldwyn-Mayer, the leading motion picture company at the time. Screenwriting was more lucrative than writing potboilers, and he took the studio jobs whenever he needed money. At various times, he also worked for Warner Brothers and Twentieth-Century Fox, and he sold the movie rights to *Sanctuary* to Paramount Studios. Unimpressed by celebrities, Faulkner met the famous actor Clark Gable, who took Faulkner hunting. Gable asked Faulkner for advice on which fiction writers were good to read, and Faulkner named several, including himself. Gable asked him, "Oh, do you write?" and Faulkner replied, "Yes, and what do you do?" For twenty years, Faulkner periodically went to California to work, usually alone, for a few weeks or months at a time. He came to hate these trips for what he saw as the superficiality of California in general and of screenwriting in particular. On one of his last trips, he observed that in Europe people asked him what he thought, but in California people asked where he had bought his hat.

## DEATH AND BIRTH

In August 1932, Faulkner's father died, leaving his oldest son the head of the family, a responsibility Faulkner took seriously. He was the son, father, brother, and uncle who gave emotional and financial support to the Falkner clan, a role that diverted attention from his writing and required him to earn more money. After his brother Dean was killed in an airplane accident, he cared for Dean's widow and daughter, and eventually paid for his grown niece's wedding and gave away the bride. After his father's death, he supplemented his mother's income with a hundred dollars a month. He treated Estelle's children from her first marriage as his own: He spent time with Malcolm and supported his interests in science, and he provided a home and emotional support for Cho Cho when her first husband left her with a small child. When Mammy Callie died, Faulkner arranged the funeral, read the eulogy, and erected a marker engraved with the words, "MAMMY Her white children bless her." His generosity showed a tender, kind nature seemingly at odds with the rough, aloof exterior that he also displayed.

In June 1933 his daughter Jill was born. Thirty-six at her

birth, Faulkner doted on the child, teaching her to ride horseback, reading to her, telling her stories. Biographer Joseph Blotner describes Jill's affection for her father:

> She loved being with him, listening to him read to her, loving the flow of the words even when she didn't understand them. Years later she would recognize the sound and rhythm of something she knew she had never read, and it would be the Dickens or Swinburne or Housman she had heard in her childhood.

Twice he brought Estelle and Jill to California with him

*As a diversion from writing, Faulkner liked farmwork at Roan Oak and Greenfield Farm.*

on screenwriting trips. But though Faulkner was devoted to Jill and catered to her wants, his attention did not always fulfill her needs. Her childhood was often lonely and hard since both of her parents drank, and sometimes both were unavailable because of their bouts with alcohol or when they traveled.

## A GROWING REPUTATION

By the time Jill was born, Faulkner had published three major novels—*The Sound and the Fury*, *As I Lay Dying*, and *Sanctuary*—and written *Light in August*, which was published in October 1932. *Light in August* was widely reviewed as the work of a major writer. Henry Seidel Canby of the *Saturday Review* called it obscure but "a novel of extraordinary force and insight, incredibly right in character studies, intensely vivid, rising sometimes to poetry." The local Oxford *Eagle* described it as Faulkner's greatest work and acknowledged the author's international fame for his earlier novels. Besides publishing a book of poems, *A Green Bough*, he sold two stories in 1933, followed by three new novels, *Pylon*, *The Unvanquished*, and *Absalom, Absalom!* When he had trouble with the first draft of *Absalom, Absalom!* he set it aside for a time and nearly rewrote it before sending it to the publisher. In 1938, he sold rights to *The Unvanquished* to MGM for twenty-five thousand dollars.

By the fall of 1935 Faulkner enjoyed a national reputation as an acclaimed writer. Publisher Bennett Cerf of Random House wanted exclusive rights to publish Faulkner's work and wrote to him: "I think we'd rather have you on our list than any other fiction writer living in America." He told Faulkner that Random House was prepared to meet his price or make an offer so good that Faulkner could not refuse it. Then in 1936, *Absalom, Absalom!* was published. Cerf praised the book as "the greatest thing you have ever turned out." One reviewer called Faulkner "a lyric poet" and another called the book his "most impressive novel." Years later Cleanth Brooks called it "perhaps his supreme story of the human heart in conflict with itself." When celebrity brought tourists down his driveway for a look at the famous author, he bought more land around his house and built a wall to keep gawkers away. As a further retreat from fame, he bought a farm among the hill people he had been writing about. Called Greenfield Farm, it was a working farm where he worked in the fields, tended animals, and fulfilled his role as a traditional Falkner farmer.

## STRESSES AND OUTLETS

Faulkner was an intense man who often felt the stress of conflicting duties to his family and to himself. He responded to stress sometimes by drinking and sometimes with behavior that strained his closest relationships. Faulkner's relationship with Estelle had been strained almost from the start; she was impatient with the inconvenience of restoring Rowan Oak and wanted fun and parties and affection. Faulkner wanted to stay home and write; he was preoccupied and unaffectionate, he worked on his farm, and he was often gone to California or New York for weeks at a time. On one of his California trips, Faulkner met Meta Carpenter, a woman whose outlook resembled his, and began a relationship that lasted intermittently over a period of fifteen years. Estelle, who knew of her husband's relationship with Meta, offered Faulkner a divorce, which he refused. Eventually, Estelle sought treatment for her drinking, accepted her husband's behavior, and realized he would never offer her the kind of living she enjoyed. Despite the conflicts, the marriage held together, and the couple found greater companionship in their later years.

At other times, Faulkner responded to stress by indulging in strenuous physical activities and risky behavior. Years after his Royal Air Force experience, he took flying lessons, bought his own plane, and took it to air shows. Because he had taught his brother Dean to fly and had sold Dean his plane, he felt guilty and responsible for Dean's airplane accident and death. He tried sailing, sometimes in risky weather. From the time Phil Stone had initiated him into the annual hunting trip, Faulkner spent a week every fall in tents with other men hunting. As head of the family, he felt obligated to lead the camp long after he no longer wanted to shoot any animal. From the days in his father's livery stable, he trained and rode horses. At Rowan Oak, he had two wild horses he was determined to break, outlaws that gave him many falls and a bad back. In later years in Virginia, Faulkner learned by sheer grit to ride in the Virginia foxhunts and jump fences and hedges. When he fell, he got back onto the horse regardless of his pain. While these activities may have served as a relief from the intensity of writing and the stress of earning money, he also found them a source of material for his stories.

## NATIONAL ATTENTION

In the late 1930s and early 1940s, Faulkner published three new novels. *The Wild Palms*, out in early 1939, juxtaposed two stories with opposite male characters. *Time* magazine gave it a good review and put his picture on the front cover, publicity that boosted sales and royalties. In March 1940, *The Hamlet* was published, the first of a trilogy planned to develop the Snopes family. He then worked on *Go Down, Moses*, a novel in seven stories, which he dedicated to Mammy Callie. He sold one of the stories, "The Bear," to the *Saturday Evening Post* for a thousand dollars in the fall before the book was published in 1942. Now that his reputation had spread beyond fellow writers and the critics, national magazines—*Life*, the *New Yorker*, *Newsweek*—took an interest in his private life, the kind of intrusion he hated. He resisted as best he could because he wanted the focus to be his books, saying that his epitaph should read merely, "He made the books, and he died."

Influential critic Malcolm Cowley wrote to Faulkner in 1943 with an idea for an article he wanted to publish. Cowley thought that a wide gap existed between writers' admiration for Faulkner's work and publishers' belief that the work would never sell. Cowley's essay, published as "William Faulkner's Human Comedy" in the *New York Times Book Review*, "declared that no living American author could match him [Faulkner] for intensity and scope." In the essay, he observed that nearly all of Faulkner's works were out of print. Cowley persuaded Viking Press to publish a collection of Faulkner's work with his introduction, entitled *The Portable Faulkner*. Faulkner drew a map of Yoknapatawpha County to include in the collection, which was published in April 1946. Faulkner liked it and told Cowley, "The job is splendid. . . . But even if I had beat you to the idea, mine wouldn't have been this good. By God, I didn't know myself what I had tried to do, and how much I had succeeded." This book prompted a number of new editions of out-of-print works.

Two books published in 1949 and 1950 brought Faulkner good fortune. In *Intruder in the Dust*, a story about Lucas Beauchamp, introduced in *Go Down, Moses*, Faulkner reveals his willingness to speak out about race and other social issues. The book received good reviews, and sold fifteen thousand copies. MGM bought the film rights to *Intruder* for fifty thousand dollars and filmed it in Oxford in the spring of 1949. Faulkner helped cast local merchants and officials in bit parts and coached outsiders on the correct southern accent. On Sunday night, October 9, amid blue-white beams of searchlights and the rousing marches of the Ole Miss band, a proud Oxford hosted the film's premiere, the Faulkner clan, dressed in their finest clothes, seated in the front rows. In 1950 *The Collected Stories of William Faulkner* was chosen as fiction alternate by the Book-of-the-Month Club. After Cowley had persuaded Random House to publish the Viking Modern Library editions, Faulkner's works sold more than a hundred thousand copies.

## THE NOBEL PRIZE FOR LITERATURE

On November 10, 1950, Faulkner received a phone call from Swen Åhman, New York correspondent for the Swedish newspaper *Dagen Nyheter*, who told him the Swedish Academy had awarded him the Nobel Prize for literature. The academy's official announcement explained that Faulkner would receive the 1949 award, which had gone unconferred in that year. At first Faulkner declared that Stockholm, Sweden, was too far away for him, a farmer, to accept the award in person, but his family persuaded him to go by telling him Jill wanted to attend. For the December ceremony, Faulkner refused to shave and wore his stained, torn trench coat with a silk top hat, a gesture characteristic of Faulkner's self-conscious eccentricity. Faulkner filed in with his fellow laureates and sat next to Bertrand Russell, recipient of the 1950 prize for literature. As described by biographer Joseph Blotner, when it came Faulkner's turn, the presenter called him the

> "unrivaled master of all living British and American novelists as a deep psychologist" and "the greatest experimentalist among twentieth-century novelists." At the fanfare of the Royal Swedish Symphony Orchestra, the whole audience rose as Faulkner stood and walked to the edge of the platform. But then, instead of descending the four steps to receive the diploma and medal and congratulations from the king, Faulkner froze. King Gustav Adolf, large and commanding, quickly walked to him and presented the award. This was apparently noticed by few, for to some, Faulkner appeared the most graceful of all the laureates as he made his bows.

At the evening banquet, each laureate gave a speech.

Faulkner delivered his standing too far from the microphone and speaking too rapidly, and the audience could not understand his southern accent. Not until the next day, when the speeches were published, did anyone realize he had delivered a great speech. It has since been called the best speech ever given at a Nobel dinner. After a round of social events, Faulkner was ready to go on to Paris with Jill when he discovered he had mislaid his Nobel medal; his valet found it in one of the potted plants.

Faulkner arrived home to a welcome by the high-school band and a full-page ad paid for by Oxford merchants. His name had been added to the city water tower, which now read "Oxford, Home of Ole Miss and William Faulkner." He accepted only an invitation to speak to members of the farm bureau, to whom he told what he had learned about Swedish agriculture from his conversation with the king. He directed his uncle, a judge, to distribute the thirty-thousand-dollar Nobel Prize cash, which he considered unearned, to benefit the poor people in Lafayette County and to boost the careers of promising Oxford blacks. Many praised his humility and generosity, but those who disliked him before disliked him still. Faulkner wrote in a letter:

> I fear that some of my fellow Mississippians will never forgive that 30,000$ that durn foreign country gave me for just sitting on my ass writing stuff that makes my own state ashamed to own me.

Receiving the Nobel Prize by no means marked the end of Faulkner's writing career. *Requiem for a Nun*, which was made into a stage play, was published in 1951. Faulkner had been working for years on an idea based on Jesus, his death and resurrection, and finally published it as *A Fable* in 1954. He continued to work on the trilogy of the Snopes family, publishing *The Town* in 1957 and *The Mansion* in 1959. (*The Hamlet* had been published in 1940.) His last book, *The Reivers*, published in 1962, was lighter and more adventurous, prompting one critic to compare him to Mark Twain. It was his nineteenth novel.

## LIVING WITH FAME

Fame brought requests for Faulkner to give speeches and lectures. He gave the commencement addresses at Jill's high school graduation and college graduation, where he echoed themes from his Nobel speech, and agreed to a series of lectures at the University of Oregon and Montana State University. In 1955 the State Department sent Faulkner around the world on a goodwill trip, during which he gave literary lectures in Japan, Manila, Paris, London, and Iceland. Scheduling Faulkner to speak carried an element of risk, however; program organizers could never be certain he would be sober enough to deliver his speech or avoid offending his hosts with outspoken remarks. Yet, on that long trip, Faulkner charmed and humored his audiences, and they accepted him with praise and applause.

Faulkner received numerous national and international prizes besides the Nobel Prize. In America, he received the William Dean Howells Medal for distinguished work in fiction, the National Book Award for fiction, and the gold medal for fiction from the National Institute of Arts and Letters. For the novel *A Fable*, he received both the National Book Award and the Pulitzer Prize. The French made him an Officier of the French Legion of Honor, and in Athens he received the Silver Medal of the Greek Academy. In Caracas, Venezuela, he received the award of the Order of Andrés Bello, the highest decoration given to a civilian, and delivered his acceptance speech in Spanish.

International fame and work never superseded Faulkner's devotion to his daughter, Jill. In March 1954 Jill wrote to her father while he was traveling in Europe and Egypt, asking him to come home because she planned to marry and her fiancé wanted her parents' consent. Jill wanted to marry Paul Dilwyn Summers Jr., an army lieutenant and Korean War veteran. When told that Jill was the daughter of William Faulkner, Paul had asked, "Who's he?" With him, Jill felt she could escape the limelight of her father's fame and find the love and security she felt she lacked in her home. On August 21, Faulkner performed all of the duties expected of the father of the bride at the wedding ceremony at St. Peter's Episcopal Church in Oxford and at the reception at Rowan Oak afterward. Jill and Paul, now discharged from the army, moved to Charlottesville, Virginia, where Paul was enrolled in the University of Virginia Law School. The birth of Jill and Paul's two sons, Paul D. Summers III and William Cuthbert Falkner Summers, gave Estelle and Faulkner reason to spend time in Virginia and impetus for Faulkner to accept a two-year post as writer-in-residence at the University of Virginia when it was offered in 1957. In 1960 Faulkner's mother died. Without the responsibility of his mother's care and in light of the hostility that Mississippians still felt toward him, he and Estelle were no longer as closely tied to Oxford as they had once been, and they moved to Charlottesville to be near their grandsons. They kept Rowan Oak, however, and often traveled between their two homes.

## SPEAKING OUT ON SOCIAL ISSUES

Despite a busy life with grandchildren, two homes, lecture assignments, and writing, Faulkner found time to speak out on social issues. He spoke against the injustice of accusing and punishing innocent blacks, and he supported the civil rights movement. On the issue of integrated education, he urged slow progress that would avoid violence and give southern blacks and whites time to learn to get along peaceably "for survival as a people and a nation." He felt that education was crucial if the lives of blacks were to improve. For his outspoken views, Mississippians labeled him a "Communist" and a "nigger-lover." Faulkner also spoke against American materialism at home and abroad. After a 1953 *Life* story covered his personal life, he said:

> What a commentary. Sweden gave me the Nobel Prize. France gave me the Legion d'Honneur. All my native land did for me was to invade my privacy over my protest and plea. No wonder people in the rest of the world dont [sic] like us, since we seem to have neither taste nor courtesy, and know and believe in nothing but money and it doesn't much matter how you get it.

On his travels to Japan, Greece, and South America as a goodwill ambassador for the State Department, Faulkner was determined to show foreigners that Americans were more than materialistic opportunists, that Americans were educated, cultured, and polite. From the responses he received from host nations, he succeeded.

Faulkner's decline came unexpectedly in July 1962. He had been spending leisurely time at Rowan Oak in June, working with Stonewall, one of the two wild horses he had brought from Oklahoma. On June 17, Stonewall spooked and threw him, and Faulkner landed at the side of the road on his already injured back. The horse nuzzled him and took off, and Faulkner limped home, got back on Stonewall, and rode him over the jumps. For two weeks, his condition worsened. The local doctor gave him pain medication but

Faulkner refused to go to the clinic until July 5, when the pain became unbearable. When he checked in at Wright's Sanitarium at Byhalia, his vital signs tested normal, and the doctor started treatment the next day. In the early hours of July 6, Faulkner sat up on the side of the bed, groaned and fell over, and could not be revived, the victim of a blood clot and subsequent heart attack. On Saturday morning, July 7, calls and telegrams came from President Kennedy and fellow writers, followed in the next days by letters from around the world. By noon on Saturday, family and friends began arriving for the simple Episcopal funeral conducted in the parlor at Rowan Oak and burial in the local cemetery. Forty-three years earlier, Faulkner had anticipated his end in these words: "the moment, instant, night: dark: sleep: when I would put it all away forever that I anguished and sweated over, and it would never trouble me anymore."

# CHAPTER 1

# Major Themes and Techniques in Faulkner's Works

# Faulkner's Portrayal
# of the South

Michael Millgate

Michael Millgate argues that William Faulkner is a
regional writer who creates a setting that reflects the
South but makes no attempt to record the actual
geographical or social history of the place. Created
from the people and images he knew in his native
Mississippi, Faulkner's Yoknapatawpha County is
his invention, as he calls it "a cosmos of my own,"
that suits the artistic purpose of his work. As a
regional writer, Millgate maintains, Faulkner is free
to reflect on hopes and despairs common to all
people. Michael Millgate was born in England, became a Canadian citizen, and has taught in England,
the United States, India, and Canada. He has written
three books about William Faulkner and books on
American fiction and British novelist Thomas Hardy.

Earlier this week I gave a lecture on Faulkner and History
which argued that history was not very important to him. . . .
"I'm inclined to think that my material, the South, is not very
important to me," wrote Faulkner to Malcolm Cowley in
1944. "I just happen to know it and don't have time in one
life to learn another one and write at the same time." And he
continued, with what for him was an unusually bitter version of that universalist view, that perception of human nature as essentially the same in all times and places . . . :
"Though the one I know is probably as good as another, life
is a phenomenon but not a novelty, the same frantic steeple-
chase toward nothing everywhere and man stinks the same
stink no matter where in time.". . .

This attitude towards the South is one which Faulkner
pretty consistently maintained, and it is of course essential to
his whole stance as a regional novelist. I stress it at this point

Excerpted from "Faulkner and the South: Some Reflections" by Michael Millgate, in
*The South and Faulkner's Yoknapatawpha: The Actual and the Apocryphal*, edited by
Evans Harrington and Ann J. Abadie. Copyright 1977 by the University Press of Mis-
sissippi. Reprinted by permission of the University Press of Mississippi.

as a way of demonstrating the inadequacy of the view, still cherished in some quarters, that Faulkner was essentially a simple country boy unaccountably struck by the divine fire—and with some fluctuations of current—and that he wrote of his native environment, its obsessions, and its problems, not out of choice but out of necessity, because he could do no other.

## The Relationship Between the Artist and His Region

Of course, I'm not saying that the divine current didn't strike, nor that Faulkner's rootedness in his native soil isn't a source strength. I *am* suggesting, however—as others have already done—that the country boy was neither so simple nor so instinctively taken up with specifically local concerns. Indeed the extent to which Faulkner felt the artist in him to be at odds with the Southerner in him emerges almost violently from a draft introduction to *The Sound and the Fury,* written in the early 1930s but published only [in the late 1970s], in the *Mississippi Quarterly:*

> Because it is himself that the Southerner is writing about, not about his environment: who has, figuratively speaking, taken the artist in him in one hand and his milieu in the other and thrust the one into the other like a clawing and spitting cat into a choker sack.[1] And he writes. We have never got and probably will never get, anywhere with music.... We need to talk, to tell, since oratory is our heritage. We seem to try in the simple furious breathing (or writing) span of the individual to draw a savage indictment of the contemporary scene or to escape from it into a make-believe region of swords and magnolias and mockingbirds which perhaps never existed anywhere. Both of the courses are rooted in sentiment; perhaps the ones who write savagely and bitterly of the incest in clay-floored cabins are the most sentimental. Anyway, each course is a matter of violent partizanship, in which the writer unconsciously writes into every line and phrase his violent despairs and rages and frustrations or his violent prophesies of still more violent hopes. That cold intellect which can write with calm and complete detachment and gusto of its contemporary scene is not among us; I do not believe there lives the Southern writer who can say without lying that writing is any fun to him. Perhaps we do not want it to be.

The legend of Faulkner the obsessive Southerner, like other legends about Faulkner, may have gained currency because it was easier to think of him that way—easier than trying to come to terms with him as he really was, as a well-read,

---

1. a gunnysack, a grain bag made of burlap

highly sophisticated, and extraordinarily conscientious literary artist. No one who knows anything of Faulkner's biography can doubt for a moment that he reached, early on, a firm and subsequently unswerving determination to become an artist, and there is evidence enough that he early assumed in full measure what some would call his arrogance, what it might be fairer to call assurance, or at least the necessary arrogance of a dedicated writer. . . .

Faulkner's use of the South as the raw material of his fiction was a matter of deliberate choice, that he adopted from the beginning a specific literary attitude towards that material, and that his sense of its possibilities grew steadily as he himself grew in stature and experience and wisdom. Yoknapatawpha County did not just happen, or simply accommodate itself to the circumstances of the place in which Faulkner happened to live. It was invented, fabricated whole, in accordance with the perceived needs of its inventor. It is not a geographical or sociological or even historical expression but a pure literary creation, not real estate but *paysage moralisé*.[2] . . .

The regional novelist in his role as pastoralist[3] is not to be confused with the local colour or dialect writer; as we have already seen, he is not concerned to present his region as it actually is, in all its crowding particularity, but to select just such details as will project a convincing image of a world which, while richly and vividly suggestive of a regional actuality, is in fact his own creation—separate, symbolic, unique. This is the process which Faulkner, in the *Paris Review* interview, called "sublimating the actual into apocryphal."[4] It is significant, for example, that Faulkner, like Hardy, makes no attempt to reproduce dialect, to play phonetic games, but only to suggest it, lightly and deftly, by the occasional introduction of local words and idioms. The most we can ask of any novelist, I suppose, even the specifically social or historical novelist, is not that he show us the way things actually are or were, but that he persuade us to see them his way. And Faulkner does this so marvellously, so deliberately, that there is a very real sense in which we not only can but should take our knowledge of the South from Faulkner's own work, since it is with that private world, not

---

2. literally, a moral landscape   3. one who portrays rural life   4. that which is widely taken to be true without proof

with the public world we call the South, that the student of Faulkner must ultimately be concerned. . . .

Jefferson isn't in the end Oxford, but a country of the mind. As Ishmael said of Queequeg's[5] native country: "It is not down on any map; true places never are." The implications, however, of recognizing Yoknapatawpha as an essentially fictional creation are very considerable. It means first of all, that there is absolutely no reason why Faulkner should have felt obligated to maintain fidelity to historical, sociological, geographical, or political fact, and that there are no grounds upon which we can properly criticize him for failing in such fidelity. That point has perhaps been sufficiently made by now. It also means that we have no grounds for assuming that any detail of the fiction is present for historical, sociological, geographical, or political reasons. *Go Down, Moses* is probably as close as Faulkner ever came to writing a conventional historical novel. "Was" presents us with a marvellously rendered image of a particular time and place, a sense of what it must or might have been like to live then and there. "The Old People" and the early parts of "The Bear" offer evocations of kinds of American experience once commonplace yet now gone forever. . . .

## SOUTHERN TRUTH TOLD THROUGH IMAGES AND EXAMPLES

While Faulkner may properly be turned to by historians in search of vivid representations of past modes of living and thinking, it cannot legitimately be asked of him, or of any serious artist, that he present a comprehensive portrait of any period, or that he make his statements about the past in specifically historical terms. . . . Faulkner, again like any serious writer, must be humbly approached and fully apprehended as an artist, a novelist employing an extraordinary range of complex fictional techniques, before he can be plundered as a source of historical or sociological statements. We have heard, for example, a complaint that Faulkner made no attempt to write about the physical brutality involved in slavery. But no one here, surely, can doubt for a moment Faulkner's absolute abhorrence of slavery and all that it was and meant.

One can certainly agree that Faulkner remained in some degree, could not but remain, the product of his own back-

5. Ishmael and Queequeg are characters in Herman Melville's novel *Moby-Dick*

ground and time. But artists speak more truly in their work, very often, than in their own persons. . . . Because Faulkner was not an historian or a polemicist but a great novelist, he sought not comprehensive documentation but moving images and representative examples. So, in *Go Down, Moses,* he focuses upon the specifically sexual exploitation involved in old Carothers McCaslin's relationships with Eunice and Tomasina, knowing full well that no episode could convey more powerfully the human degradation implicit in the whole system of slavery—present no less strongly when slaves were what is called well-treated than when they were beaten. And the episode, because it is so movingly created for us, not directly presented but growing to gradual horrific realization within Ike's mind and within the reader's own mind as both move through the entries in the commissary books, documents made eloquent by their very inarticulateness as they occur on pages otherwise so richly written—the episode haunts our memories as an image of the inhumanity not just of slavery itself, not just of those other varieties of sexual exploitation, . . . but of all forms of exploitation of human beings by other human beings. . . .

## FAULKNER'S FOCUS ON A MOMENT AND A PLACE

The wonderful particularity of Faulkner's realizations is precisely the source of the strength which makes his images available, accessible, as embodiments of universal truths. Yoknapatawpha, the specifically regional world, serves as a kind of organizing principle for this Faulkner particularity, and it is perhaps worth repeating, at this moment and in this place, that joyful account of the invention and elaboration of Yoknapatawpha which comes at the end of the *Paris Review* interview, itself one of the most deliberate non-fiction statements about himself and his art which Faulkner ever made. Someone [has] asked what one should do when one ran into difficulties when reading a Faulkner novel, and [the lecturer] very properly replied: "Read it again." I would simply add to that Faulkner's advice about Joyce:[6] that he should be read with faith, as the Baptist preacher does the Bible. Faulkner himself has to be read with that kind of faith, and as I read out a passage that I know must be familiar to all of you, I have the sense almost of reciting a creed:

6. Irish novelist James Joyce, who also used internal monologues in his novels

Beginning with *Sartoris* I discovered that my own little postage stamp of native soil was worth writing about and that I would never live long enough to exhaust it, and by sublimating the actual into apocryphal I would have complete liberty to use whatever talent I might have to its absolute top. It opened up a gold mine of other peoples, so I created a cosmos of my own. I can move these people around like God, not only in space but in time too. The fact that I have moved my characters around in time successfully, at least in my own estimation, proves to me my own theory that time is a fluid condition which has no existence except in the momentary avatars of individual people. There is no such thing as *was*—only *is*. If *was* existed there would be no grief or sorrow. I like to think of the world I created as being a kind of keystone in the universe; that, as small as that keystone is, if it were ever taken away, the universe itself would collapse. My last book will be the Doomsday Book, the Golden Book, of Yoknapatawpha County. Then I shall break the pencil and I'll have to stop.

What I want to register on this occasion, is above all the exultation audible here, the justified pride in achieved purpose. . . .

It is also important, however, to take note of that claim of total power over his created universe which Faulkner here advances, and which is really all the response that is needed to complaints about the inconsistencies as between one book and another. . . . I mean, of course, those minor inconsistencies which came from his returning to characters and events used in previous books but not checked out in those books before he used them again—not just because he hated to go back to what he'd written before, because he wanted always to be moving onwards, but simply because those characters and those events had continued all the time to exist and flourish, fully active, in his own imagination. As Faulkner quietly insists in that prefatory note to *The Mansion*: "The author has learned, he believes, more about the human heart and its dilemma than he knew thirty-four years ago; and is sure that, having lived with them that long time, he knows the characters in this chronicle better than he did then." Even the Creator, after all, didn't get his world fixed right on the first day but went on making improvements over the next five, having lived with it that long time and knowing its characteristics better at the end of the week than he did in the beginning. William Faulkner, I think, may therefore be allowed his thirty-odd human years of progressive development and discovery, a brief enough span after all. . . . He managed to create a body of literature, a broad shelf of books, such as no other twentieth-century American novelist has equalled, and which precious few writers anywhere, at any time, in any language, have surpassed.

In New Orleans Faulkner had promised, or threatened, that he could compete with Shakespeare if he cared to do so. Thirty years and twenty-odd books later he could speak with splendid confidence of having created a cosmos of his own, a world that could be thought of as a kind of keystone in the universe. Indeed, his exuberance throughout the *Paris Review* interview, his sense of having matched himself against the best throughout his career, is so marked as to make one wonder whether in using the term "apocryphal" he didn't also intend to suggest that if his own work was not holy writ, it was certainly the next best thing.

# Faulkner's Novels Are Experimental

## Maxwell Geismar

Maxwell Geismar characterizes William Faulkner
as an experimental novelist whose use of internal
monologue and symbolism creates an ambiguity
that allows multiple levels of meaning, at once
expressing the plight of the isolated individual and
criticizing society. Specifically, Geismar explains,
Faulkner's stories and characters portray the decaying agrarian South in the early twentieth century
and the rise of commercialism in the region. Maxwell
Geismar, who taught at Sarah Lawrence College in
New York, was a writer, lecturer, historian, and critic.
He wrote seven books on American literature and
edited many more.

Born in 1897, a year later than Dos Passos and Fitzgerald and
a year earlier than Hemingway,[1] the young William Faulkner
shared in the common experience of his generation: he
joined the Canadian Flying Corps and served with the R.A.F.
in France. In him, too, the variety of its origins helped to explain the variety of the American genius. Faulkner was heir
to a family of Southern governors, statesmen, and other public figures; early in his childhood he went to live in Oxford,
Mississippi, and it was his home almost uninterruptedly
thereafter. . . .

Faulkner built his work on an even grander scale than Dos
Passos. He related even his minor personages with one another, he elaborated their genealogy from generation to generation, he gave them a countryside: a deep land of Baptists,
of brothels, of attic secrets, of swamps and shadows. "Jefferson," Mississippi, is the capital of this world which reaches

1. American novelists John Dos Passos, F. Scott Fitzgerald, and Ernest Hemingway

Reprinted with the permission of Simon & Schuster from Maxwell Geismar's "A Cycle
of Fiction," in *Literary History of the United States*, Revised Edition, by Robert E.
Spiller, Willard Thorp, et al. Copyright 1953 by Macmillan Publishing Company; copyright renewed ©1981 by Robert E. Spiller and Willard Thorp.

backward in time to the origins of Southern culture and forward to the horrid prophecies of its extinction, and which
ranges down in social strata from dying landed aristocracy,
the Sartoris and Compson families, to the new commercial
oligarchy of the Snopeses;[2] down to the poor-white Bundrens
of *As I Lay Dying,* to the pervert Popeye of *Sanctuary,* and to
the Negro Christmas of *Light in August,* turned brute again
by the society which had raised him from the animal.

## TWO EXPERIMENTAL NOVELS

It is typical of Faulkner's meteoric talent that the three years
between 1929 and 1932 contain two of his major works, *The
Sound and the Fury* and *Light in August.* Both novels are
highly experimental in form. As a matter of fact, all of
Faulkner's big novels are marked by a technical experimen-
tation which adds to an already formidable ambiguity of
content. *Light in August* (1932), probably the most easily
comprehensible to the average reader, seems to be written
as an objective narrative; but it holds tale within tale and its
meaning becomes clear only if you follow the story of Lena,
the poor-white mountain girl—and a Faulknerian symbol of
a rather appalling, blind, lower-class sexual fertility—to the
story of Hightower, isolated, sterile, living in his memories
of the Old South. Underneath, is the story of the New South:
the murder in Jefferson, Mississippi, and the love affair of
the northern spinster, Miss Joanna Burden, with the mulatto
Christmas. Here finally Faulkner gives expression not only
to the most bitter and profound cultural problem of the
South, but to its dominant cultural phobia; and the night-
marish quality is matched only, perhaps, by one's sense of
its reality in the haunted minds of the central figures.

The Faulknerian dialectic,[3] which became reasonably
clear in *Light in August,* had already been suggested in *The
Sound and the Fury* (1929). The earlier novel is even more
complex in its technique. It is an outstanding example of the
interior monologue[4] in our letters; and the skill of its archi-
tecture—the style moves from almost complete obscurity to
the statement of prosaic fact—is evident in the use of the
unifying symbols: the circus tickets, the river, the broken

2. Sartoris, Compson, and Snopes are family names in Faulkner's novels   3. intellectual investigation by means of discussion and reason   4. the record of the internal,
emotional experience of a character on any one level or on combinations of several
levels of consciousness

watch, the tolling clock, and, indeed, all the manifestations of dissolving time that pervade the novel. It is very different from *Light in August* in tone. In the Compson children, Faulkner caught the torment of childhood at the moment it reaches maturity—at the moment, that is, of the realization of sin and evil, the moment of the "Fall." Thus the "incestuous" love of Quentin Compson for his sister Caddy, which forms the central theme and provides the most eloquent passages of the novel, and which Faulkner handles with a peculiarly touching naivete, is incestuous merely because these legitimate feelings of childhood—in a sense, the only true feelings of childhood—are judged from outside, from an adult framework of values. Indeed, filled as the tale is with all the pathetic devices and drives and tensions of infancy, and the intimations of those other lawless and poignant affections which color the better—or the worse—part of our lives, *The Sound and the Fury* is matched by few novels in its evocations of infantile origins. In spite of being specialized in form, rather self-consciously limited in appeal, it was a landmark of the new literature.

But the childhood here revealed is in a sense a double one. The drama of innocence and corruption takes place within a larger framework: there is the conflict, again, of a decaying landed aristocracy with the rising commercial classes. Avaricious and bigoted, the Jason Compson of *The Sound and the Fury is* the protagonist of the new economic order which, in effect, closes the novel. And, by contrast with Jason's "practicality," even the idiot Benjy Compson, whose obscure moaning and slobbering opens the novel, is an intelligible hero.

## FAULKNER REPRESENTS A CHANGING SOUTH

At least that is what Faulkner seemed to suggest, as he compared the youth of his culture with its misbegotten maturity. In the series of grotesque legends which followed, *As I Lay Dying* (1930), *These 13* (1931), *Sanctuary* (1931), and his later novels and tales, Faulkner dealt with the New South—with this modern stage, on which strut only those modern personages whose milieu is a cold and calculating corruption, whose single instinct is a lust for power, and whose lares and penates[5] are the Faulknerian "Snopeses." It was

---

5. treasured household possessions, historically household gods; the suggestion is that modern southerners worshiped the Snopses and aspired to be like them

only in *Absalom, Absalom!* in 1936, that Faulkner seemed to regain something of the tone of *The Sound and the Fury;* but there again he was treating the rise and decay of a landed aristocracy—and there, too, Quentin Compson proclaimed that he did not hate the South. "'I dont hate it,' he said. *I dont hate it* he thought, panting in the cold air, the iron New England dark; *I dont. I dont! I dont hate it! I dont hate it!"*

With William Faulkner, the cultural pattern of isolation, of revolt, and of denial, the heritage of the American twenties lasting over and fully forming the American novelist of the 1930's reached an extreme. Here the two main elements of the pattern—the solitary and desperate individual of Hemingway's work, the acrid and despairing critique of contemporary society in Dos Passos' work—are given fullest expression, while even the shimmering flappers of Fitzgerald become a type of Faulknerian incubus. Indeed, the "misty tragedy" played far behind the veil becomes rather more explicit, and the sense of latent horror in the earlier evocation of the Jazz Age becomes acute. There is no denying Faulkner's real achievement. In the scope of his scene and the dimensions of his portraiture, in the complexity and subtlety of his emotions, as well as in the vivid and complex prose style, he is perhaps, as Gide remarked, *"the* most important of the stars in this new constellation." Nor is this Mississippi symbolist quite so esoteric as he may seem at first; for his picture of the Mississippi Valley and its people is the work of a realist even when, with the Representative Rankins, the Snopeses go to Washington. Those who praise Faulkner indiscriminately, *Sanctuary* as well as *The Sound and the Fury,* are in a sense unaware of how good Faulkner can be, and to what degree the history of this remarkable talent is also the history of its dissipation. The increasing stress on technical virtuosity, the sacrifice of content for effect, and of effect for shock—these, too, show the destructive element at work.

# Humor in Faulkner's Works

Harry Modean Campbell and Ruel E. Foster

Harry Modean Campbell and Ruel E. Foster argue that humor is an important element in all but a few of William Faulkner's stories and novels. The authors define and provide numerous examples of two major kinds of humor—surrealistic and frontier—and explain the function and effect of each. Harry Modean Campbell has written biographies of historical and political figures as well as other critical works on American authors. Ruel E. Foster has taught English at West Virginia University at Morgantown and published two books, *Elizabeth Madox Roberts: American Novelist* and *Jesse Stuart*, as well as numerous articles, poems, and stories in literary journals.

[A] major element of Faulkner's art is his humor. It is extremely important in accounting for the unique effect of his fiction, and humor appears as an influential norm in all of his major works except *Absalom, Absalom!* Little systematic analysis of this humor has been made; yet a knowledge of it—or at least a feel for it—is indispensable for any reasonably complete reading of Faulkner's works. Faulkner, himself, writing in an essay published in 1926, comments on the importance of humor in this manner:

> We have one priceless trait, we Americans. The trait is our humor. What a pity it is that it is not more prevalent in our art. This characteristic alone, being national and indigenous, could, by concentrating our emotional forces inward upon themselves, do for us what England's insularity did for English art during the reign of Elizabeth. One trouble with us American artists is that we take our art and ourselves too seriously.

Some initial difficulty, however, is encountered in defining humor. We may say, provisionally, that the essence of humor lies in incongruity, which arises when a person mentally jux-

Excerpted from *William Faulkner: A Critical Appraisal* by Harry Modean Campbell and Ruel E. Foster. Copyright 1951 by the University of Oklahoma Press. Reprinted by permission of the publisher, the University of Oklahoma Press.

taposes two experiential contexts and notes an inconsistency and disproportion between them. The resulting experience will not always be what we call humor; yet when humor occurs it always begins in some such disparity. It may be genial and kind humor or harsh and sadistic. It may involve both conscious and unconscious levels of experience. In the sense that it is an affective state, it is immediate and ultimate. Some such provisional definition as this will be most helpful in taking hold of what is important in Faulkner's humor.

Aside from some early imitative humor, we can distinguish two major variations or modes of humor in Faulkner: surrealistic[1] humor and frontier or native Southern humor. . . . Of greater importance is a more unusual kind of humor, associated with the numerous elements of the subconscious in Faulkner's works, that may be described as "surrealistic," a type of atrabilious[2] humor which differs qualitatively from traditional native Southern humor. We may also borrow from the surrealists two terms which suggest the nature of this qualitative difference:

1. Alienation of sensation—meaning a startling juxtaposition of seemingly incongruous images, a deliberate defiance of familiar or logical associations that leads to the viewpoint Kenneth Burke calls "perspective by incongruity." To some extent this perspective operates in all humor; it interests the surrealists when the incongruity arises from the yoking of two radically different categories. . . .

2. Black Bile—supposedly the laughter of the unconscious—a disagreeable, cruel laughter. Distortions and the grimaces of extreme pain are funny. Black Bile evidences the power of the id which has no regard for the humanitarian dictates society thrusts upon the ego. Black Bile is sadistic.[3] . . .

### EXAMPLES OF SURREALISTIC HUMOR

Turning to *Sanctuary,* we may take, then, as an example of surrealistic humor, the funeral scene of the young gangster, "Red." As the chapter opens, Red's expensive black and silver coffin is disclosed on the dance floor of a cheap roadhouse outside Memphis. The reader is then committed to a scene which is a macabre parody of a conventional funeral. The

---

1. having a dreamlike or unreal quality; attempting to express the subconscious; characterized by imagery   2. melancholy, peevish, surly   3. These two definitions are paraphrased from Herbert Muller, "Surrealism, A Dissenting Opinion," in *New Directions, 1940,* ed. by James Laughlin.

alienation of sensation derives from the juxtaposition of two experiential contexts which are, in terms of authority, contradictory. Authority through taboo and religion invests a funeral with an aura of decorum, awe, and piety; in this scene, convention is symbolically raped by placing the funeral in the licentious, riotous, transient atmosphere of the roadhouse. The scene develops by a series of correspondences which cumulatively step up the force of this alienation. Notice these couplings which give the scene the effect of a macabre double-focus: The nightclub—(church) holds the coffined body of Red—(the faithfully departed) attended by gangsters and prostitutes—(mourners) listening to a bootlegger—(minister) deliver a drunken eulogy (funeral sermon).

From this incongruous scene, perspectives radiate to our modern funeral customs—the evangelical burial services, or the materialism of our idealism. . . . A touch of the sadism of Black Bile is added by a drunken brawl which thrusts Red's corpse suddenly out of the coffin onto the floor with an air of comic somnolence, while a wire from the flowers pierces the cadaver's cheek.

From this example, we can indicate the minimum ingredients of a surrealistic humor situation:

1. Some object, belief, or custom, reverenced by convention (authority).

2. Some incongruity yoked to the above which violates the reverence.

3. The psychic state resulting when the subject apprehends and reacts to the above situation. Sadism (Black Bile) enters in to the extent to which the violence is seriously meant by the instigator. . . .

Faulkner's short story, "A Rose for Emily," provides a classic example of the grim humor fascinating the surrealist. All the ingredients of surrealistic humor are in it. The reverential connotations cluster about romantic love, the bridal night, and Southern womanhood. By the incongruous juxtaposition of murder and the image of a woman who passes her bridal night in the arms of her murdered lover and later sleeps with his rotting corpse, these hallowed clusters are brutally violated. The iron-grey hair resting on the pillow by the corpse serves as an objective correlative[4] precipitating

---

4. a situation or a sequence of events or objects that evoke a particular emotion in a reader or an audience

the ambivalent emotional state with which we react to the situation—we are both attracted and repelled. We view with loathing the grisly trappings of fleshly decay, but are drawn perversely back with a shocked fascination to the image of Miss Emily and her incredible perversity in bedding with a corpse. Having seen Miss Emily through the story as the town saw her for many years, a strange but harmless eccentric, we now suddenly see behind the mask, as it were, and the entire anterior action of the story appears suddenly, spatially, in a new and now grisly perspective. It is grimly humorous in retrospect to think of the city fathers, sitting in the parlor of a murderess, mumbling apologetically about her past taxes until she dismisses them contemptuously from the house in which the decaying corpse of her lover even then rests unperturbedly in the upper room. . . .

## THE EFFECTS OF SURREALISTIC HUMOR

Scenes and language examples like the foregoing can be found with considerable frequency in most of Faulkner's books, particularly in *The Sound and the Fury, As I Lay Dying, Light in August, Pylon,* and "Miss Zilphia Gant." Because of its frequency and effectiveness, such surrealistic humor is obviously quite important, and its general effect upon the total character of his writing may be summarized briefly as this: First, scenes like those quoted from *Sanctuary,* by their discreteness and discontinuity and difference from the texture of the rest of the novel, tend to give a rather dissembled, illogical, dream quality to sections of a particular novel. Secondly, unless the surrealistic humor is relieved by the more natural, pleasant, Southern frontier humor, the story suffers; "Miss Zilphia Gant" is an example here. On the other hand, the effect of surrealistic humor becomes greater if emphasized by a contrasting, opposite kind of humor, as in *Sanctuary,* in which the Snopeses provide broad, comic relief. Lastly, this type of humor very definitely imparts a distinct grotesquerie to parts of Faulkner's work.

## THE TECHNIQUES OF SOUTHERN FRONTIER HUMOR

The other major mode of humor in Faulkner, the Southern frontier humor, has appeared in his novels since the publication of *Sartoris,* at least, and it assumes a greater importance as he grows older. Faulkner employs all the techniques associated with frontier humor—the tall tale, dialectal variations, hyperbole, understatement, obscenity, Aesopian animal humor, trick situations, Negro humor, and so on.

*The Hamlet,* which contains much surrealistic humor, is also filled with native frontier humor. (Phil Stone, to whom *The Hamlet* is dedicated, maintains that he and Faulkner worked up the Snopes saga together in a spirit of anecdotal whimsy. Models were at hand in and about Oxford, and they began to contrive comic situations for them; from this material grew the novel. According to Mr. Stone, at least three new characters will appear in a later version of the Snopes saga—"Dollar Watch" Snopes, "Montgomery Ward" Snopes, and "Admiral Dewey" Snopes, the latter called "Ad.") In *The Hamlet,* Faulkner's overall conception is broadly comic, often Rabelaisian.[5] The controlling comic situation derives from a conflict between an established power—the Varners— and an incipient threat to this power—Flem Snopes. Since the Varners are rather tight-fisted themselves, the reader has the traditional comic experience of seeing the cheater cheated, as Flem gradually outwits the Varners. Paralleling Flem's rise to power is the appearance of one after another of the Snopes clan, who pop up with comic and inexplicable suddenness within the village until Jody Varner feels he is being drowned under a great tide of Snopeses. To complete the comic inversion of fortunes, we see, in the last scene of the book, the seemingly infallible Ratliff, through sudden cupidity, become a complete dupe of Flem. Thus Flem triumphs over all. However, a word of qualification is needed here. As the comic inversion of fortunes is completed and Flem emerges triumphant, the humor is complicated by the presence of the surrealistic elements in the idiot-cow love scene. In this, Flem acquires a darker aspect to his character: frog-like, he emerges as a brutal but coldly calculating monster of greed. And yet he has a broadly comic side. A balance of such discordant elements is seldom achieved, and the fact that Faulkner does achieve it in *The Hamlet* accounts for the unique tone of the story.

A situation which verges on the Rabelaisian is provided by Mrs. Varner. . . . Jody Varner has just discovered that his unmarried sister Eula is pregnant, and he storms angrily into the house. He is loudly rebuffed by the father, and into the hurly-burly steams Mrs. Varner, gasping angrily from

5. characterized by coarse humor, exuberance, or bold caricature

her mountainous flesh, "Hold him till I get a stick of stove wood. . . . I'll fix him. I'll fix both of them. Turning up pregnant and yelling and cursing here in the house when I am trying to take a nap!" It is obvious that interrupting Mrs. Varner's nap is Eula's chief sin. An important thing to note here is the function of the humor; in this scene the comedy works to transform the effect of Jody's jealousy of his sister. Essentially Jody throughout the story has been as careful and as jealous of his sister's sexual honor as Quentin was of that of his sister Caddy. However, Quentin's reaction to Caddy's indiscretion was morbid and suicidal, whereas Jody's is one of loud and angry frustration, comic to the audience. Faulkner's emphasis on comedy here effectively negates the melodramatic pressures which would otherwise threaten throughout the scene.

Caricature, a salient characteristic of frontier humor, appears in many forms throughout *The Hamlet,* and it is apparent in what might be called Faulkner's name-humor: the name of a character is chosen to suggest his paramount quality. The name "Snopes," for instance, suggests in its curt shortness some of the vulgar Anglo-Saxon monosyllables. The initial letters, "Sn," in fact, have many unpleasant connotations. About fifty per cent of the words beginning with "Sn" in Webster's *Unabridged Dictionary* have disagreeable connotations (snake, snarl, sneer, snivel, snob, and so on). "Snopes," then, is a caricature of all "Sn-ishness" in human nature. Beginning with this surname, Faulkner goes on to caricature the particular qualities of "Sn-ishness" possessed by each of the Snopeses.

Most important of all is Flem Snopes—the bellwether of the clan. The name suggests two things to us. In the terminology of I.A. Richards, Flem, as a "sense" metaphor, suggests "phlegmatic"; as an emotive metaphor, it suggests phlegm (phonetically spelled "flem" in the dictionary). Both fit Flem's character. The medieval humor, phlegm, when predominant, made a person cold, apathetic, unemotional— so Flem—phlegmatic. As a mucous discharge from the mouth, it bears further revolting connotations.

The name-humor is further complicated by the introduction of animal nicknames, suggesting Aesopian animal characteristics, and grandiose Christian names negated by the incongruous nicknames. Here is the roll call of the remaining Snopeses with their accompanying animal quality:

1. Flem Snopes (froglike)
2. I.O. Snopes, the platitudinarian[6] (weasel)
3. Lancelot (Lump) Snopes (ratlike)
4. Ike H. Snopes, the idiot (bovine)
5. "Mink" Snopes, the murderer
6. St. Elmo Snopes—omnivorous, huge, fleshy, beastlike
7. Wallstreet Panic Snopes (son of Eck)
8. Montgomery Ward Snopes ⎫ to be developed in
9. Dollar Watch Snopes      ⎬ subsequent stories
10. Admiral Dewey Snopes    ⎭

The obvious humorous leads given by these names are exploited obviously in the narrative in manners too detailed to be followed, but it should be apparent that the quality of Snopes animality is the primary element of caricature here—this is Faulkner's oblique version of Aesop's "The Fox and the Raven" or of Uncle Remus' "Brer Rabbit and Brer Fox.". . .

In *The Sound and the Fury*, Faulkner's fourth novel, Jason, cold, self-centered, and pragmatic, speaks his monologue, in the third section, very much like a Ring Lardner character. Consider his opening paragraph—an address to his mother about his niece:

> Once a bitch, always a bitch, what I say. . . . I says she ought to be down there in that kitchen right now, instead of up there in her room, gobbing paint on her face and waiting for six niggers that can't even stand up out of a chair unless they've got a pan full of bread and meat to balance them, to fix breakfast for her.

This is characteristic of the rather rough, sardonic tone Jason maintains throughout; all of his comments are well sprinkled with caustic wisecracks. Here is one prompted by the death of his father, who died a chronic alcoholic: "Like I say, if he [father] had to sell something to send Quentin to Harvard we'd all been a damn sight better off if he'd sold that sideboard and bought himself a one-armed strait jacket with part of that money." In the same vein is his remark about his castrated idiot brother, "I could hear the great American Gelding snoring his head off." This semihumorous, caustic tone continues up to the last sentence of Jason's section—a sardonic jab at the Negroes on his place.

## USE OF BOTH SURREALISTIC AND FRONTIER HUMOR

*As I Lay Dying* utilizes both surrealistic and frontier humor in its picture of a poor white family taking with great diffi-

---

6. one who habitually makes trite or banal remarks as if they were original or significant

culty the decaying corpse of their mother by wagon to a distant burying ground. The initial scene has the macabre air of a medieval Dance of Death painting. As it opens, Addie Bundren, the mother, is dying. Outside her window, in full view and sound of the dying woman, her oldest son Cash, a carpenter, is making her coffin. The hammering and sawing sounds come flooding into the window and from time to time Cash holds up a choice board for his mother to admire. As a foil to this grotesquerie, we get the coarseness of Dewey Dell's (note the name) reference to Doc Peabody as "that old green-eating tub-of-guts"; Anse's statement at the death of his wife, "God's will be done . . . now I can get them [store] teeth"; Anse's lugubrious comfort for Cash, "Lucky Cash broke the same leg twice"; and Anse's final speech which can be read as pure farce. At the cost of all the anguish and turmoil related in the novel, the Bundrens have fulfilled Anse's oath to his wife to bury her properly. On the same afternoon of the burial, Anse returns to the family, waiting patiently on the wagon in the public square; he names each of the children in turn—It's Cash and Jewel and Vardaman and Dewey Dell." Then pointing to a low, waddling woman by his side, "Meet Mrs. Bundren," he says. The tremendous understatement of this conclusion inevitably calls up the story *Old Man,* in which a convict in a boat is cast out on the Mississippi River in the worst flood in history and battles up and down it for six weeks. When the flood is over, he rows back to the levee he had started from, finds an officer, and surrenders, merely saying—"Yonder's your boat, and here's the woman. But I never did find that bastard on the cottonhouse."

*Sanctuary* gets its broad comic relief from the Snopeses who are so countrified that they spend two weeks in a Memphis bawdyhouse thinking it's a hotel until their cousin Clarence enlightens them. Clarence then takes them to a Negro bordello, which is cheaper, remarking as he holds up a dollar bill—"This stuff's color blind." *Absalom, Absalom!* lacks all traces of this frontier humor, and therein lies one of its major flaws. In *Wild Palms* we have two separate novelettes. The first one, *Wild Palms,* is unrelieved by humor and is a very poor story. The second, *Old Man,* shows many characteristics of the humorous tall tale and is a much superior story. *The Unvanquished* makes humor out of the Civil War through the McCaslins, the Negroes, and the boy protagonist.

## Two Functions of Humor

We may say, then, that humor functions generally in two fashions in Faulkner's works: first, in a structural sense—that is, it may contribute an additional conflict to the plot and it may serve to balance other conflicts in the plot; and second, in an atmospheric sense—that is, it gives, in the case of frontier humor, a softness, a bearableness, or a more diffused focus to a scene which otherwise might well be starkly tragic, melodramatic, or overemotional. Surrealistic humor, on the other hand, tends to create an atmosphere of whim, perversity, caustic irony, or Swiftian bitterness, adding a darker undercurrent to a scene which might be sheer slapstick on the surface. It does this by evoking multiple and contradictory emotions simultaneously. . . .

As an illustration of structural frontier humor on a large scale, we can cite the story of Lena Grove in *Light in August.* There are three nodes of interest in *Light in August*—one centering around Joe Christmas, one about Reverend Hightower, and one about Lena Grove. Two are stories of frustration ending in violent death, the third—of Lena Grove and Byron Bunch—a pastoral idyl ending in a presumably rewarding future. This latter story, which is basic to the total plot of the novel, is conceived comically from the very beginning when we are told that Lena's illegitimate pregnancy is due to the fact that she learned to raise the window in her room and had raised it once too often. The situation could easily have fallen into pathos or bathos if Faulkner had chosen to emphasize the piteousness of this poor, pregnant girl, making a long journey on foot, without friends or money, into an alien country in fruitless search of a faithless and worthless lover. But as the story progresses, we see that the traditional view does not apply at all to Lena: she overcomes obstacles with ease. When she finally reaches Jefferson, she descends from the wagon, looks about, and remarks with dead-pan peasant understatement, "Here I aint been on the road but four weeks, and now I am in Jefferson already. My, my. A body does get around."

The author's purpose, a comic inversion of values, is evident: the betrayed and ingenuous country girl (so typed ) who suddenly becomes not an object of pity and concern, but an actual tower of strength about whom the persevering forces of the story gather. This is the basic incongruity. But this comic pastoral contains other values as well: it fits into

Faulkner's general scheme of emphasis on the superiority of rural primitive virtues over urban, decadent ones (a system best exemplified by "The Bear"); and throughout the story the chaotic, hopeless life of the introspective, cultured, neurotic Hightower and the introspective, cheap, urban, fated life of Joe Christmas are held in ironic contrast to the inner serenity and certitude of the primitive, rural girl, Lena Grove....

Finally, we must consider the atmospheric function of Faulkner's humor, the use of humor to give an emotional ambivalence to a scene—the guarded style. A classic example of this is contained in what is probably Faulkner's most important long short story, "The Bear." This story is a rather complicated one concerning the consciousness of Isaac McCaslin as he matures and learns the primitive mysticism of the wilderness and the ancient guilt which lies upon the bloodline of his family. One of the important—and for the boy, tragic—scenes of the book is the one in which he learns that his grandfather, old Carothers McCaslin, has been guilty of both incest and miscegenation. He has fathered a child by a slave and then has had incestuous relations with his own mulatto daughter. The boy learns this indirectly through the crudely humorous and laconic entries in an old plantation ledger which dates back before the Civil War. Here is the entry (in his father's hand):

> *Eunice Bought by Father in New Orleans 1807 $650 dolars.*
> *Marrid to Thucydus 1809 Drownd in Crick Cristmas Day 1832.*

and then the other hand appeared . . . his uncle's . . .

> *June 21th 1833 Drownd herself*

and the first:

> *23 Jun 1833 Who in hell ever heard of a niger drownding him self*

and the second hand, unhurried with a complete finality . . . :

> *Aug 13th 1833 Drownd herself*

Eunice, who drowned herself, was Old McCaslin's first Negro mistress and it was her daughter (by McCaslin) who was involved in the incest. This knowledge, disclosed with Olympian casualness by the ledger entries, is tremendously unsettling for the boy. But the involved ledger entries, odd spelling, and the laconic dialect humor help underplay and protect the scene from open emotionalism. Thus the horror of incest and miscegenation is presented, and presented realistically and skillfully by tempering it in the fashion noted above. At the same time, as the scene is finished, a delayed reaction comes, in which, for some people, the horror may be increased by the very casualness of the humorous contrast offered.

Faulkner, then, we see, is a writer who conceives his stories in a complicated mood—a mood for the most part generously salted with humor. His humor may be cruel and sadistic, or it may be genial and anecdotal, or it may, and often does, mingle both the cruel and the genial. In his best work, the humor is almost always an integral part of the experiential context of the narrative—it is very seldom exploited for its own sake. Faulkner is not primarily, however, a humorous writer, but he is a writer with a unique sense of humor which is used to give new perspectives into the meaning of the human experience he is portraying.

# Faulkner's Use of Motion as Metaphor

Richard P. Adams

Richard P. Adams bases his critique on Faulkner's belief that the artist's purpose is to arrest motion, or life. Adams defines and provides examples of four techniques Faulkner uses to freeze a moment, in which one thing contradicts another: violence, time management, counterpoint, and imagery. Richard P. Adams has taught at Rutgers University and Tulane University and been a Fulbright lecturer in France. In addition to articles in scholarly journals, Adams has published a novel, *The Eden Affair*.

William Faulkner had an exceedingly large and complex mind, and a creative genius that assimilated the most astonishing amount and variety of cultural materials into itself and the work it produced.... This study does not pretend to explain all aspects of Faulkner's writing. Its focus is narrow and its approach is only one of many that may be profitable. But I believe that it strikes somewhere near the center of what Faulkner tried to do and did do.

The basic hypothesis of my investigation is expressed in two statements made by Faulkner in 1954, in an interview with Jean Stein for the *Paris Review*. He said that "Life is motion" and that "The aim of every artist is to arrest motion, which is life, by artificial means and hold it fixed so that a hundred years later, when a stranger looks at it, it moves again since it is life." These two apparently simple remarks imply a profound and complex attitude toward the world and man's destiny, which requires for its expression a difficult esthetic doctrine and an elaborate exercise of artistic and technical discipline.

My belief is—and my hypothesis therefore holds—that Faulkner had this attitude from the beginning of his career, that he learned what it meant and what it demanded esthetically, and that in time he developed adequate strategies and techniques to embody it in his fiction. . . .

## THE DIFFICULTIES OF PRESENTING LIFE AS MOTION

The proposition that "Life is motion" committed Faulkner to the imagination of a world in which the concrete experience of humanity is continual change. Such a world is extremely hard to conceive, and quite impossible to formulate, because all formulas are static. If life is motion, always changing, never the same in any two views or moments, it cannot be directly represented in a work of art or logically explained in a philosophical or critical essay. Every statement about its concrete manifestations is false because, by the time the statement has been made and heard, the object has become something else, the relationships between the object and the observers have shifted, and the maker and the hearer of the statement have themselves whirled onward, not to return.

Faulkner therefore is not trying to formulate experience in any direct or logical way. He is trying to organize impressions of speed and energy in order to build the most intense possible concentrations of force, and then to confine them in the most tightly blocked possible situations. The phrase "to arrest motion" is a rather tricky paradox, if motion is what is to be represented; but it is a paradox imposed by the nature of the problem. Because motion cannot be directly described, it must be demonstrated indirectly by the static "artificial means" the artist has to work with. If we conceive of motion as a stream (an image often used by Faulkner) we find that its power cannot be felt by someone moving with it, or in it, as living people normally do. If, however, some object, or better, if some person, can be made to stand still against its flow, the result will be a dramatic and possibly disastrous manifestation of its energy.

## VIOLENCE AS A TECHNIQUE

Faulkner commands a wide variety of techniques, and some of them are more positively dynamic than his statement of the artist's aim would strictly seem to allow. His use of violence, for example, involves both a negative and a positive aspect. Its purpose is not merely to shock the reader, much less to cater to a sadistic fascination with the horrible for its own sake, as some early detractors assumed, but rather to dramatize the unquenchable vigor of life by showing it in the act of overwhelming and crushing static obstacles in its path. The accompanying imagery generally tends in one way or another, or in several ways at once, to build up a feeling of tremendous force and speed. Flood, fire, wind, stampeding animals, moving crowds of people, burgeoning vegetation, hot sunshine, odors of growth and decay, flocks of birds, and swarms of buzzing insects carry the sense of universal motion in hundreds of scenes where potential or actual violence is, as Faulkner once remarked, "the by-product of the speed and the motion. . . ." The violence is inevitable and necessary, as the obstacles are, to show the power in concerted action. The strategy is especially successful when it involves great suffering on the part of a character who has the reader's sympathy.

It is in aid of this strategy that some of Faulkner's most static and intrinsically least attractive characters, such as Popeye in *Sanctuary,* Joe Christmas in *Light in August,* and Jason Compson in *The Sound and the Fury,* are given attributes which make them parallel to Christ. Conversely, some of the most attractive characters, many of whom are also Christlike, such as Ike McCaslin in *Go Down, Moses,* Horace Benbow in *Sanctuary,* and Jason's brother Quentin in *The Sound and the Fury,* are also among the most static; they are more effective as instruments of Faulkner's purpose only because we care more what happens to them. Quentin is the most effective of all, for most readers, because he is so sensitive, so naïvely innocent, so intelligent, and so completely and inevitably doomed. He is driven to suicide by his inability to accept the illegitimate pregnancy of his sister Caddy, and more generally by his revulsion from any kind of mature sexual activity. Mr. Compson, his father, points out that pregnancy is a particularly vital manifestation of the motion of life through time, remarking quite rightly that "It's nature is hurting you not Caddy"; and Quentin is driven all the harder toward his death by his realization of this truth. Time, as Mr. Compson also remarks, is Quentin's "misfortune" because he is hysterically determined not to accept the complications of mature behavior. The only way he can preserve his youthful innocence is to die. Horace Benbow, Joe Christmas, and Ike McCaslin are faced with similar dilemmas, but their fate is less clear and somewhat less deeply moving because they compromise. They accept maturity and then find that they cannot cope with the problems and responsibilities that it brings.

## THE COMPRESSION OF TIME AND THE USE OF COUNTERPOINTS

Another technique that Faulkner uses to concentrate the motion of life is his management of time. Conventionally, we think of narrative as being more or less chronological, and in the actual world we think of motion as taking place in four dimensions, of which the dimension of time is perhaps the most important, as well as the most difficult to get hold of in terms of either concrete sensual impressions or abstract logical thinking. Intuitively, we are aware of time going on, and of temporal relations among events as they happen. But Faulkner often departs from a straight chronological presentation in his fiction, and, by a calculated scrambling of the time dimension, short-circuits our intuition so as to concentrate the energy of a large amount of motion on a single, artificially fixed and isolated moment. When it succeeds, this technique may have the effect of compressing a lifetime into a single event. The scrambling prevents our feeling time as a thin, straight string with events marked off at measured intervals; instead, we feel it as a heavy cluster, knot, or tangle, with all the ends lost in the middle. Motion is lost, or stopped, and time is held still for esthetic contemplation.

A closely related technique is Faulkner's use of "counterpoint," that is, the juxtaposition or alternation of superficially unrelated matters in such a way that esthetic tensions build up between or among them. When Faulkner defined the term most clearly, he was talking about *The Wild Palms,* in which two completely separate series of events take place, in alternate chapters, throughout the novel, which he nevertheless insisted was "one story—the story of Charlotte Rittenmeyer and Harry Wilbourne, who sacrificed everything for love, and then lost that." But this story had a fatal tendency to run down, and whenever it did, Faulkner said, "I wrote on the 'Old Man' story until 'The Wild Palms' story rose back to pitch." The two stories are completely separated in time and space, they have no characters in common, and their thematic relations are not obvious. However, after much discussion and argument, most critics now seem to feel that the book as Faulkner published it, and claimed he composed it, is better than either of its parts alone, although it is still not regarded as one of Faulkner's best.

Counterpoint works in more complex ways toward more impressive results in some of Faulkner's other novels. The three main stories that make up *Light in August* are hardly more closely tied than the two in *The Wild Palms;* and the four narrators of *The Sound and the Fury* are so different in attitude, temperament, and point of view that they give quite different accounts of the situation. Similar effects are achieved by the several narrators of *As I Lay Dying* and *Absalom, Absalom!,* by the various points of view in *The Hamlet,* and by the assembly of loosely related stories in *Go Down, Moses.* All these devices serve the same purpose. Their presentation of sharply separate views, which become simultaneous in the reader's mind, makes it possible for Faulkner to arrange his static impressions of moving life in clusters and patterns that heighten both the motion and the stasis, an effect that would be spoiled if the parts were more smoothly articulated.

Another effect that Faulkner often gets from the contrapuntal juxtaposition of incongruous materials is a lusty, wild, and frequently violent humor. . . . The result is not tragedy, or even merely pathos, but, as Hoffman[1] also remarks, "a uniquely comic view of life and an optimistic conviction of human destiny." The frequent savagery of Faulkner's humor, instead of preventing, actually enhances the optimistic outcome. The appalling hardships which are overcome by his comic heroes, such as the Bundrens (except Darl), the tall convict in *The Wild Palms,* and Mink Snopes, together with the inordinate amounts of energy they spend against the obstacles in their way are proof, in the end, that man will prevail in spite of everything. The more pathetic and absurd their predicaments become, the more triumphantly the power of life asserts itself in their survivals and their often ridiculous victories.

## FAULKNER'S SOURCES

Much of the material that Faulkner used to construct his works was borrowed or, as he preferred to say, stolen from other authors, whose monuments he looted as ruthlessly as the popes did those of ancient Rome, and for purposes as

1. critic Daniel

foreign to their original intent. From his richest mine, the King James Bible, his favorite story was that of Christ's Passion; but he also referred often to the story of Eden, and occasionally to those of Abraham and Isaac, David and Absalom, Joseph and his brothers, and many more. Another great store was classical mythology, which Faulkner found not only in Homer, the Greek playwrights, and the Latin poets, but also in the works of classical anthropologists such as Sir James Frazer, Jane Harrison, and Gilbert Murray. . . .

---

### A PAUSE WHILE CATCHING A HORSE

*In* As I Lay Dying, *Jewel Bundren and his horse stand together in a moment when Faulkner's description freezes their motion.*

When Jewel can almost touch him, the horse stands on his hind legs and slashes down at Jewel. Then Jewel is enclosed by a glittering maze of hooves as by an illusion of wings; among them, beneath the upreared chest, he moves with the flashing limberness of a snake. For an instant before the jerk comes onto his arms he sees his whole body earth-free, horizontal, whipping snake-limber, until he finds the horse's nostrils and touches earth again. Then they are rigid, motionless, terrific, the horse back-thrust on stiffened, quivering legs, with lowered head; Jewel with dug heels, shutting off the horse's wind with one hand, with the other patting the horse's neck in short strokes myriad and caressing, cursing the horse with obscene ferocity.

They stand in rigid terrific hiatus, the horse trembling and groaning. Then Jewel is on the horse's back. He flows upward in a stooping swirl like the lash of a whip, his body in midair shaped to the horse. For another moment the horse stands spraddled, with lowered head, before it bursts into motion. They descend the hill in a series of spine-jolting jumps, Jewel high, leech-like on the withers, to the fence where the horse bunches to a scuttering halt again.

---

In addition, he was saturated with talk, which is still an artistic medium in north Mississippi, and from which, as he said in an interview or two, he got much of his awareness of the traditions, legends, and what we may call the mythology of the South. He used this material in the same way as he used the Bible and the classical mythology, as a thief by sovereign right, and often with scant respect for the pieties in which it might be invested by conventional people.

The contrapuntal method works in a somewhat special way, in Faulkner's fiction as in that of Joyce[2] and in the poetry of Eliot,[3] when it is used on materials taken from traditional, legendary, mythological, and literary sources. These materials bring some of their own connotations with them, and represent their own times. When we find them in a modern work, and especially when several of them appear side by side, a startling sense of temporal dislocation may arise. When a character is made to look like Christ, or when, in *The Hamlet,* Eula Varner is characterized as the Helen of Frenchman's Bend and the idiot Ike Snopes falls gallantly in love with Houston's cow, Houston himself being something of a cross between a knight and a centaur, or when Quentin Compson in *Absalom, Absalom! is* haunted to the point of being possessed by the aristocratic ghosts of Civil War soldiers, the resulting intrusion of the Biblical, the classical, the feudal, or the American legendary past into the modern situation contradicts the flow of time and provides an artificially static moment into which Faulkner can compress great quantities of life. . . .

## THE USE OF IMAGERY TO FREEZE A MOMENT

The arrest of motion is accomplished most often and most directly in Faulkner's work by imagery in which the dynamic quality of life is immediately and sharply opposed to artificial stasis. This device creates the "frozen moment" that has been defined and studied by several critics. Examples are far too numerous to list, but we may note a few, by way of random illustration. They occur in Faulkner's early work in such images as that of the statue in the garden in *The Marble Faun,* and in the description of an equestrian statue of Andrew Jackson in "Out of Nazareth," one of the sketches written in New Orleans in 1925, where horse and rider are seen "in terrific arrested motion." In *As I Lay Dying* the same effect is achieved more vividly by a description of living figures when Jewel Bundren catches his horse and holds it "rigid, motionless, terrific" before mounting to ride. The same kind of imagery occurs in connection with the death of Joe Christmas in *Light in August.* It is used in the passingly noticed vision of a man, a mule, and a plow in *In-*

2. Irish novelist James   3. American poet T.S.

*truder in the Dust,* and in the account of Boon Hogganbeck's
tremendous efforts to get an automobile out of a mudhole in
*The Reivers.* The point in each of these passages, and in
many others where such imagery occurs, is the contrast it
contains between an aspect of speed or intense effort, representing motion, and an opposing aspect of impediment or
countering force that stops the motion or slows it so much
that it seems to stop. . . .

## THE RELATIONSHIP BETWEEN MOTION AND MORALITY

The moral implications of Faulkner's world of motion have
not been well understood by most critics. Many have assumed that he is describing a static world, in which life
would be impossible, and these have logically concluded
that the only moral outcome is despair. Even after the Nobel
Prize speech, many have been content to adopt the term "endure" as the key to Faulkner's meaning. But in the speech, in
many interviews, and in all his artistic works, if we read
them rightly, Faulkner has said that "man will not merely
endure: he will prevail." What Faulkner liked to call not
virtues but "verities . . . of the heart" were such as "love and
honor and pity and pride and compassion and sacrifice," all
of which he conceived in active terms. His most completely
defeated characters, such as Quentin Compson, Horace Benbow, or Joe Christmas, go down because they are funda-
mentally opposed to life. They try to find something un-
changing to stand on, motionless in the midst of change. But
motion sweeps them on so relentlessly that their only escape
is one or another kind of suicide. They are not vital spirits
crushed by the inert weight of matter. On the contrary, they
are desperate because a living world keeps forcing them into
action in spite of their desire for security, peace, and stasis.
They are crushed because they are trying not to move, and
because, by Faulkner's logic, the only way to be motionless
is to be dead.

They and others like them are Faulkner's most useful
characters because they provide the most dramatic contrasts
between the motion of life and the static obstacles that, by
opposing, demonstrate its power. They serve their purpose
best, as we have seen, when they most engage the reader's
sympathy. But they are not morally admirable. On the other
hand, characters such as Caddy Compson, Ruby Lamar, and
especially Lena Grove are so much in harmony with the mo-

tion that they, by themselves, could hardly show it at all. Their moral and esthetic value can be dramatized only by contrast with static characters such as Quentin, Horace (or Popeye), and Christmas.

In an effort to represent morally admirable qualities of human nature more directly, Faulkner invented another kind of character, so conceived that he has to learn the value of life, more or less against his inclinations, and, by hard struggle, ally himself with it actively in the effort to overcome whatever obstacles may be. Byron Bunch in *Light in August*, Chick Mallison in *Intruder in the Dust*, the battalion Runner in *A Fable*, and Lucius Priest in *The Reivers* are perhaps the handiest examples, in that they most clearly represent the learning process, which is an excellent image of dynamic energy working against the drag of ignorance and sloth. V.K. Ratliff, the sewing machine agent, is morally active and admirable in *The Hamlet, The Town,* and *The Mansion;* but he is not as effective as the others in a dramatic way because he seems more fully armed from the start, and has less painful development to undergo. In general, the better Faulkner's characters are in their moral alliance with life or in their natural adjustment to its pace and rhythm, the less they are able to do for the esthetic success of his work. Those who serve him best are the discontented, the maladjusted, the desperate, and the morally bad.

## FAULKNER'S CREATION OF YOKNAPATAWPHA COUNTY

Faulkner's greatness as the creator of a world and as the chronicler of its legendary history has tended, in the minds of some critics, to obscure his greatness as an artist, that is, primarily as a novelist. But Yoknapatawpha County would never have been more than potentially interesting or important if it had not been embodied in successful works of art. Its whole existence, now that Faulkner is dead, is in the works; and we may reasonably assume that it might never have existed except as a way to make them possible. It is not untrue to say, as Malcolm Cowley does in his introduction to *The Portable Faulkner,* that the works were carved out of an amazingly large and complete conception in Faulkner's mind, and that they are somewhat arbitrarily separated fragments of a whole that must have been greater than their sum. But I prefer to emphasize the opposing view, which Faulkner often suggested, that the world of Yoknapatawpha grew as the works were created, and because they were created. This view permits us to regard the individual novels as organically complete works of art in themselves, without denying that their ensemble is an even larger work, which in some ways may transcend them all.

However we choose to look at it, Faulkner's work is a magnificent achievement. In each of his better novels, in many short stories, and in the total body of his fiction, we receive a profound and comprehensive impression of life. The first characteristic that distinguishes this fiction from most other literature is that, in the whole and in the parts, down to the smallest details of matter and of method, it moves. The second is that the motion is rendered visible and artistically usable by a marvelous variety of technical devices that arrest it for esthetic and moral contemplation. It comes to us as highly compressed vital energy, which we can release, if we take it rightly, to make our own lives move more widely and deeply than they otherwise might. Faulkner's greatness is that he has added life to life and a world of richly imagined motion to the moving world in which we live.

# CHAPTER 2

# Faulkner's Most Anthologized Stories

# Atmosphere and Theme in "A Rose for Emily"

Ray B. West Jr.

Ray B. West Jr.'s analysis of the atmosphere—the time, place, and conditions—in William Faulkner's "A Rose for Emily" shows that distortion results when characters confuse past and present. Seen first by the town as merely eccentric, Emily clings to the past to preserve her dignity and reputation, to the extent that she murders her lover and sleeps with his corpse. West concludes that the story illustrates Faulkner's theme: that humans must come to terms with both past and present, but when they deny either and fail, their effort to overcome their plight is heroic. Ray B. West Jr. has taught at the University of Montana in Missoula and the University of Kansas in Lawrence. He has published poems and stories in literary magazines and is the editor of *Rocky Mountain Stories* and *The Art of Modern Fiction.*

The first clues to meaning in a short story usually arise from a detection of the principal contrasts which an author sets up. The most common, perhaps, are contrasts of character, but when characters are contrasted there is usually also a resultant contrast in terms of action. Since action reflects a moral or ethical state, contrasting action points to a contrast in ideological perspectives and hence toward the theme.

The principal contrast in William Faulkner's short story "A Rose for Emily" is between past time and present time: the past as represented in Emily herself, in Colonel Sartoris, in the old Negro servant, and in the Board of Aldermen who accepted the Colonel's attitude toward Emily and rescinded her taxes; the present is depicted through the unnamed narrator and is represented in the *new* Board of Aldermen, in Homer Barron (the representative of Yankee attitudes to-

Excerpted from "Atmosphere and Theme in Faulkner's 'A Rose for Emily'" by Ray B. West, *Perspective*, Summer 1949. Reprinted by permission of the Estate of Ray B. West.

ward the Griersons and through them toward the entire South), and in what is called "the next generation with its more modern ideas."

Atmosphere is defined in the *Dictionary of World Literature* as "The particular world in which the events of a story or a play occur: time, place, conditions, and the attendant mood." When, as in "A Rose for Emily," the world depicted is a confusion between the past and the present, the atmosphere is one of distortion—of unreality. This unreal world results from the suspension of a natural time order. Normality consists in a decorous progression of the human being from birth, through youth, to age and finally death. Preciosity in children is as monstrous as idiocy in the adult, because both are *unnatural*. Monstrosity, however, is a sentimental subject for fiction unless it is the result of human action— the result of a willful attempt to circumvent time. When such circumvention produces acts of violence, as in "A Rose for Emily," the atmosphere becomes one of horror.

Horror, however, represents only the extreme form of maladjusted nature. It is not produced in "A Rose for Emily" until the final act of violence has been disclosed. All that has gone before has prepared us by producing a general tone of mystery, foreboding, decay, etc., so that we may say the entire series of events that have gone before are "in key"—that is, they are depicted in a mood in which the final violence does not appear too shocking or horrible. We are inclined to say, "In such an atmosphere, anything may happen." Foreshadowing is often accomplished through atmosphere, and in this case the atmosphere prepares us for Emily's unnatural act at the end of the story. Actually, such preparation begins in the very first sentence:

> When Miss Emily Grierson died, our whole town went to her funeral: the men through a sort of respectful affection for a fallen monument, the women mostly out of curiosity to see the inside of her house, which no one save an old manservant—a combined gardener and cook—had seen in at least ten years.

### The Contrast Between Emily's Past and Present

Emily is portrayed as "a fallen monument," a *monument* for reasons which we shall examine later, *fallen* because she has shown herself susceptible to death (and decay) after all. In the mention of death, we are conditioned (as the psychologist says) for the more specific concern with it later on. The second paragraph depicts the essential ugliness of the contrast: the description of Miss Emily's house "lifting its stubborn and coquettish decay above the cotton wagons and the gasoline pumps—an eyesore among eyesores." (A juxtaposition of past and present.) We recognize this scene as an emblematic presentation of Miss Emily herself, suggested as it is through the words "stubborn and coquettish." The tone—and the contrast—is preserved in a description of the note which Miss Emily sent to the mayor, "a note on paper of an archaic shape, in a thin, flowing calligraphy in faded ink," and in the description of the interior of the house when the deputation from the Board of Aldermen visit her: "They were admitted by the old Negro into a dim hall from which a stairway mounted into still more shadow. It smelled of dust and disuse—a close, dank smell." In the next paragraph a description of Emily discloses her similarity to the house: "She looked bloated, like a body long submerged in motionless water, and of that pallid hue."

Emily had not always looked like this. When she was young and part of the world with which she was contemporary, she was, we are told, "a slender figure in white," as contrasted with her father, who is described as "a spraddled silhouette." In the picture of Emily and her father together, framed by the door, she frail and apparently hungering to participate in the life of her time, we have a reversal of the contrast which has already been presented and which is to be developed later. Even after her father's death, Emily is not monstrous, but rather looked like a girl "with a vague resemblance to those angels in colored church windows—sort of tragic and serene." The suggestion is that she had already begun her entrance into that nether-world (a world which is depicted later as "rose-tinted"), but that she might even yet have been saved, had Homer Barron been another kind of man.

By the time the deputation from the new, progressive Board of Aldermen wait upon her concerning her delinquent taxes, however, she has completely retreated into her world of the past. There is no communication possible between her and them:

> Her voice was dry and cold. "I have no taxes in Jefferson. Colonel Sartoris explained it to me. Perhaps one of you can gain access to the city records and satisfy yourselves."

"But we have. We are the city authorities, Miss Emily.
Didn't you get a notice from the sheriff, signed by him?"
"I received a paper, yes," Miss Emily said. "Perhaps he
considers himself the sheriff.... I have no taxes in Jefferson."
"But there is nothing on the books to show that, you see.
We must go by the—"
"See Colonel Sartoris. I have no taxes in Jefferson."
"But Miss Emily—"
"See Colonel Sartoris." [Colonel Sartoris had been dead al-
most ten years.] "I have no taxes in Jefferson. Tobe!" The
Negro appeared. "Show these gentlemen out."

Just as Emily refused to acknowledge the death of her father, she now refuses to recognize the death of Colonel Sartoris. He had given his word, and according to the traditional
view, "his word" knew no death. It is the Past pitted against
the Present—the Past with its social decorum, the Present
with everything set down in "the books." Emily dwells in the
Past, always a world of unreality to us of the Present. Here
are the facts which set the tone of the story and which create the atmosphere of unreality which surrounds it.

---

### THE HORROR OF A DECAYED BODY

*After Miss Emily's funeral, relatives beat down the door to
the room no one has seen for forty years.*

The man himself lay in the bed.

For a long while we just stood there, looking down at the
profound and fleshless grin. The body had apparently once
lain in the attitude of an embrace, but now the long sleep that
outlasts love, that conquers even the grimace of love, had
cuckolded him. What was left of him, rotted beneath what
was left of the nightshirt, had become inextricable from the
bed in which he lay; and upon him and upon the pillow beside him lay that even coating of the patient and biding dust.

Then we noticed that in the second pillow was the indenta-
tion of a head. One of us lifted something from it, and leaning
forward, that faint and invisible dust dry and acrid in the nostrils, we saw a long strand of iron-gray hair.

---

Such contrasts are used over and over again: the difference between the attitude of Judge Stevens (who is over
eighty years old) and the attitude of the young man who
comes to him about the "smell" at Emily's place. For the
young man (who is a member of the "rising generation") it

is easy. For him, Miss Emily's world has ceased to exist. The city's health regulations are on the books. "Dammit, sir," Judge Stevens replied, "will you accuse a lady to her face of smelling bad?" Emily had given in to social pressure when she allowed them to bury her father, but she triumphed over society in the matter of the smell. She had won already when she bought the poison, refusing to comply with the requirements of the law, because for her they did not exist.

## THE CONTRAST BETWEEN EMILY AND HOMER

Such incidents seem, however, mere preparation for the final, more important contrast between Emily and Homer Barron. Emily is the town's aristocrat; Homer is a day laborer. Homer is an active man dealing with machinery and workmen—a man's man. He is a Yankee—a Northerner. Emily is a "monument" of Southern gentility. As such she is common property of the town, but in a special way—as an ideal of *past* values. Here the author seems to be commenting upon the complex relationship between the Southerner and his past and between the Southerner of the present and the Yankee from the North. She is unreal to her compatriots, yet she impresses them with her station, even at a time when they considered her *fallen*: "as if [her dignity] had wanted that touch of earthiness to reaffirm her imperviousness." It appeared for a time that Homer had won her over, as though the demands of reality as depicted in him (earthiness) had triumphed over her withdrawal and seclusion. This is the conflict that is not resolved until the final scene. We can imagine, however, what the outcome might have been had Homer Barron, who was not a marrying man, succeeded, in the town's eyes, in seducing her (violating her world) and then deserted her. The view of Emily as a monument would have been destroyed. Emily might have become the object of continued gossip, but she would have become susceptible to the town's pity—therefore, human. Emily's world, however, continues to be the Past (in its extreme form it is death), and when she is threatened with desertion and disgrace, she not only takes refuge in that world, but she also takes Homer with her, in the only manner possible.

It is important, too, to realize that during the period of Emily's courtship, the town became Emily's allies in a contest between Emily and her Grierson cousins, "because the two female cousins were even more Grierson than Miss

Emily had ever been." The cousins were protecting the general proprieties against which the town (and the times) was in gradual rebellion. Just as each succeeding generation rebels against its elders, so the town took sides with Emily against her relations. Had Homer Barron been the proper kind of man, it is implied, Miss Emily might have escaped both horns of the dilemma (her cousins' traditionalism and Homer's immorality) and become an accepted and respected member of the community. The town's attitude toward the Grierson cousins represents the usual ambiguous attitude of man toward the past: a mixture of veneration and rebelliousness. The unfaithfulness of Homer represents the final act in the drama of Emily's struggle to escape from the past. From the moment that she realizes that he will desert her, tradition becomes magnified out of all proportion to life and death, and she conducts herself as though Homer really had been faithful—as though this view represented reality.

Miss Emily's position in regard to the specific problem of time is suggested in the scene where the old soldiers appear at her funeral. There are, we are told, two views of time: (1) the world of the present, viewing time as a mechanical progression in which the past is a diminishing road, never to be encountered again; (2) the world of tradition, viewing the past as a huge meadow which no winter ever quite touches, divided from (us) now by the narrow bottleneck of the most recent decade of years. The first is the view of Homer Barron and the modern generation in Jefferson. The second is the view of the older members of the Board of Aldermen and of the confederate soldiers. Emily holds the second view, except that for her there is no bottleneck dividing her from the meadow of the past.

## TRADITION, DEATH, AND THE PAST

Emily's small room above stairs has become that timeless meadow. In it, the living Emily and the dead Homer have remained together as though not even death could separate them. It is the monstrousness of this view which creates the final atmosphere of horror, and the scene is intensified by the portrayal of the unchanged objects which have surrounded Homer in life. Here he lay in the roseate atmosphere of Emily's death-in-life: "What was left of him, rotted beneath what was left of the nightshirt, had become inextricable from the bed in which he lay; and upon him and upon the pillow beside him lay that even coating of the patient and biding dust." The symbols of Homer's life of action have become mute and silent. Contrariwise, Emily's world, though it had been inviolate while she was alive, has been invaded after her death—the whole gruesome and unlovely tale unfolded.

In its simplest sense, the story says that death conquers all. But what is death? Upon one level, death is the past, tradition, whatever is opposite to the present. In the specific setting of this story, it is the past of the South in which the retrospective survivors of the War deny changing customs and the passage of time. Homer Barron, the Yankee, lived in the present, ready to take his pleasure and depart, apparently unwilling to consider the possibility of defeat, either by tradition (the Griersons) or by time (death) itself. In a sense, Emily conquered time, but only briefly and by retreating into her rose-tinted world of the past, a world in which death was denied at the same time that it is shown to have existed. Such retreat, the story implies, is hopeless, since everyone (even Emily) is finally subjected to death and the invasion of his world by the clamorous and curious inhabitants of the world of the present.

In these terms, it might seem that the story is a comment upon tradition and upon those people who live in a dream world of the past. But it is not also a comment upon the present? There is some justification for Emily's actions. She is a tragic—and heroic—figure. In the first place, she has been frustrated by her father, prevented from participating in the life of her contemporaries. When she attempts to achieve freedom, she is betrayed by a man who represents the new morality, threatened by disclosure and humiliation. The grounds of the tragedy is depicted in the scene already referred to between Emily and the deputation from the Board of Aldermen: for the new generation, the word of Colonel Sartoris meant nothing. This was a new age, a different time; the present was not bound by the promises of the past. For Emily, however, the word of the Colonel was everything. The tax notice was but a scrap of paper.

## COMING TO TERMS WITH PAST *AND* PRESENT

Atmosphere, we might say, is nothing but the fictional reflection of man's attitude toward the state of the universe. The atmosphere of classic tragedy inveighed against the ethical dislocation of the Grecian world merely by portraying

such dislocation and depicting man's tragic efforts to con-
form both to the will of the gods and to the demands of his
own contemporary society. Such dislocation in the modern
world is likely to be seen mirrored in the natural universe,
with problems of death and time representing that flaw in
the golden bowl of eighteenth- and nineteenth-century natural philosophy which is the inheritance of our times. Perhaps our specific dilemma is the conflict of the pragmatic
present against the set mores of the past. Homer Barron was
an unheroic figure who put too much dependence upon his
self-centered and rootless philosophy, a belief which suggested that he could take whatever he wanted without con-
sidering any obligation to the past (tradition) or to the future
(death). Emily's resistance is heroic. Her tragic flaw is the
conventional pride: she undertook to regulate the natural
time-universe. She acted as though death did not exist, as
though she could retain her unfaithful lover by poisoning
him and holding his physical self prisoner in a world which
had all of the appearances of reality except that most necessary of all things—life.

The extraction of a statement of theme from so complex a
subject matter is dangerous and never wholly satisfactory.
The subject, as we have seen, is concerned not alone with
man's relationship to death, but with his relationship as it
refers to all the facets of social intercourse. The theme is not
one directed at presenting an attitude of Southerner to Yankee, or Yankee to Southerner, as has been hinted at in so
many discussions of William Faulkner. The Southern Problem is one of the objective facts with which the theme is concerned, but the theme itself transcends it. Wallace Stevens is
certainly right when he says that a theme may be emotive as
well as intellectual and logical, and it is this recognition
which explains why the extraction of a logical statement of
theme is so delicate and dangerous an operation: the story *is*
its theme as the life of the body *is* the body.

Nevertheless, in so far as a theme represents the *meaning*
of a story, it can be observed in logical terms; indeed, these
are the only terms in which it can be observed for those
who, at a first or even a repeated reading, fail to recognize
the implications of the total story. The logical statement, in
other words, may be a clue to the total, emotive content. In
these terms, "A Rose for Emily" would seem to be saying that
man must come to terms both with the past and the present;

for to ignore the first is to be guilty of a foolish innocence, to ignore the second is to become monstrous and inhuman, above all to betray an excessive pride (such as Emily Grierson's) before the humbling fact of death. The total story says what has been said in so much successful literature, that man's plight is tragic, but that there is heroism in an attempt to rise above it.

# Tobe's Significance in "A Rose for Emily"

T.J. Stafford

T.J. Stafford argues that the Negro servant Tobe in "A Rose for Emily" is a counterpoint to Miss Emily, her corruption and withdrawal. In Stafford's analysis, Tobe performs useful household tasks and provides a link to the outside world; the spelling of Tobe (to be) suggests hope for a future when he is released from the decay in which he has been serving. T.J. Stafford has contributed articles on American writers to a number of scholarly journals.

In William Faulkner's "A Rose for Emily," a search for the motivation of Emily Grierson's murder of Homer Barron usually begins with an effort to understand Miss Emily herself. Until she is understood, everything remains an enigma. In trying to solve the puzzle, Brooks and Warren conclude that her behavior reflects a pride and independence of spirit which are highly regarded by Faulkner.[1] Such a view, however, fails to account for the disparity between the admirable qualities motivating the action and the ignominy of the act. To view Miss Emily in this way is to come to the story with a presupposition about what Faulkner is doing and not to look at the story as it actually operates, for the fact remains that Miss Emily's relation with Homer is an abnormal, degenerate, and meaningless human association which is unworthy of the pride it took to attain it.

In a work of art, one cannot always isolate the part he wishes to understand, for other parts may offer a necessary perspective. In this case, Faulkner's purpose becomes more clear by seeing Miss Emily in contrast to her Negro servant.

1. This story, one of Faulkner's most popular, has received many interpretations, but no one has approached it, at least in print, as it is here explicated. Brooks and Warren (*Understanding Fiction*, New York, 1959) are cited as an example of the type of readings it has had.

From T.J. Stafford, "Tobe's Significance in 'A Rose for Emily,'" *Modern Fiction Studies*, vol. 14, no. 4 (Winter 1968–69), pp. 451–53; ©1968, The Johns Hopkins University Press. Reprinted by permission of The Johns Hopkins University Press.

While Emily occupies the foreground and provides the primary movement (a movement toward decay), the servant hovers in the background and offers a countermovement of purposeful activity. Although only ten separate references are made to the Negro, each is strategically placed and richly suggestive of his contrast with Miss Emily.

## TOBE'S ACTIVITIES

Faulkner gives a rather full impression of the servant's activities. He does the gardening, marketing, and cooking, all of which sustain Miss Emily physically. He conducts the townsmen in and shows them out when she is finished with them, and later he admits Homer at the kitchen door. He is, as protector of Miss Emily, thought of as having killed a snake or a rat. He thus engages in purposeful and altruistic action. Miss Emily, by contrast, gives an impression of immobility, "motionless as that of an idol," an image which Faulkner reiterates. In only one section (III) is Emily able to perform action, courting Homer Barron, riding about town, and buying arsenic. Ironically, it is the only section in which the Negro does not appear, and Emily's one set of deeds, performed without the servant's being present in the story, results in violence and destruction.

## THE SIGNIFICANCE OF TOBE

The servant offers Miss Emily the means for contact with humanity in two ways. On the one hand, his errands furnish a link between her deteriorating world and human society, while on the other hand, he is in himself a whole and healthy human (a fact established by his ability to perform and to remain in contact with the world). But his provision for an access to the human heart for Miss Emily also contrasts with her condition. First, his sallies forth to the marketplace, his meeting the world that comes to her door (and turning it away only at her command), and his final liberation into the world after her death, all stand in juxtaposition to her isolation and alienation. Second, although he is himself a human, she does not even talk with him, for, as the narrator says, his voice "had grown harsh and rusty, as if from disuse."

The Negro servant's importance actually lies beyond the story's end. Faulkner suggests this meaning through the choice of name, "Tobe," emphasized by avoiding the usual spelling of "Toby" and clearly implying that he is "to be," that once he is liberated from the foul atmosphere of Miss Emily's alienation and paralysis his fulfillment will be. The ending reinforces this suggestion, for, while exposing Miss Emily's inability to engage in meaningful human associations, it frees Tobe from her decayed sphere into a world that is to be.

## TOBE AS SEEN IN A BROAD CONTEXT

Tobe's significance becomes even more clear in the broader frame of Faulkner's work. Dilsey is like Tobe in that she is the only person in *The Sound and the Fury* who is able to engage in meaningful action and who provides a moral center to the story. Also like Tobe, she sustains and protects her white masters, outlives them, and suggests the indomitability of the human spirit. Tobe also relates to certain views expressed by Faulkner. In *The Bear,* for example, Ike McCaslin tells Lucas Beauchamp that the white man has had his turn and that someday "your peoples' turn will come because we have forfeited ours." Later Ike says that the Negro people "will endure. They will outlast us. . . . They are better than we are. Stronger than we are." It is the same idea implied in Faulkner's Appendix to *The Sound and the Fury* which ends with the simple description of Dilsey, "they endured."

## TOBE'S SUCCESS; EMILY'S FAILURE

Tobe, like Dilsey is to the Compsons, has thus been more than a servant to Miss Emily's physical needs. While serving as cook and gardener, he has demonstrated the possibility of meaningful action; while meeting the world for her, he has provided her with the means for contact with it. But she has been unable to avail herself of his humanity and in so failing she suggests the explanation for her abnormal and depraved relation with Homer Barron, which is in itself symbolic of her relationship with the human heart, her own, Tobe's, and human kind's.

While it may be true, as Brooks and Warren say, that Emily reveals pride and independence of spirit, qualities which Faulkner greatly valued, it is even more clear that in Miss Emily they do not lead to a richer life but are perverted into destruction and decay. Thus, Faulkner here qualifies his feelings about pride, demonstrating that it is insufficient in itself and that other qualities are needed to humanize it.

These qualities are shown through Tobe who reveals humility, patience, endurance, courage, and pity. A clearer picture of Miss Emily's true nature is therefore given by her sharp contrast with Tobe's wholeness. Toward the end, a feeling of release is associated with Tobe as he disappears into the future and the narrator turns to lead the reader into the room of dust, death, and decay which Emily Grierson has created.

# "The Bear" as Allegory and Essay

Joseph Gold

According to Joseph Gold, William Faulkner's story "The Bear" is a flawed blend of allegory and essay. Gold argues that although the men and animals involved in the hunt are no more than symbols in an abstract allegory, the character of Ike is developed with human qualities characteristic of fiction. Gold thinks that in trying to blend allegorical and fictional characters, Faulkner loses the effectiveness of both. His major objection is that Faulkner's point of view directly intrudes into the story. Born in London, Joseph Gold has taught at the University of Manitoba and the University of Waterloo in Canada. He has contributed to numerous journals and edited two books on British novelist Charles Dickens.

The long short story "The Bear" illustrates perfectly the change of emphasis which has characterized Faulkner's work since 1948. "The Bear" is in many ways the turning point in the work of Faulkner, the signpost which indicates his change of direction from the creation of myth to the construction of discourse, from the play of imagination to the exercise of ratiocination. Both by its internal structure and by the history of its composition, "The Bear" reveals the tendency in Faulkner to explicit statement, to rhetoric, to monologue, and to sententiousness.[1] ... An examination of the method will show that Faulkner has adopted here the characteristics of allegory and essay and that several participants in the action are emblems rather than characters—a situation which never occurs in the work of the previous two decades. ...

A close examination of "The Bear" will reveal that it is

---

1. moralizing

Faulkner's intention here to turn legend into allegory. Faulkner begins by telling us that "there was a man and a dog too this time. Two beasts, counting Old Ben, the bear, and two men, counting Boon Hogganbeck." Faulkner would seem to imply, as early as his first two sentences, that Old Ben is not really a beast and Boon is not really a man. The word "counting" can be explained only in this way. What is Ben if he is not really a beast? He is the wilderness itself. He is a legend, a long one: "The long legend of corn-cribs broken down and rifled, of shoats and grown pigs and even calves carried bodily into the woods and devoured." He is a ferocious force devoid of malice, but unbeatable. He is "an anachronism . . . out of an old dead time." Sam Fathers, half-Indian, half-Negro, self-dedicated to the woods, knows that Ben is without sentiment and dismisses contemptuously the story that Ben takes care of the younger bears. "He don't care no more for bears than he does for dogs or men either." Ben, the "chief bear," is an essence, a distillation of the power and spirit and fate of the wilderness.

What is Boon if he is not really a man? He is a child, with the mind of a child in his man's body; he "was four inches over six feet; he had the mind of a child, the heart of a horse, and little hard shoe-button eyes without depth or meanness or generosity or viciousness or gentleness or anything else." He is childlike in the face of the complexities of civilization. With a gun he is useless. Whoever finally would shoot the bear, "It would not be Boon. He had never hit anything bigger than a squirrel that anybody ever knew, except the Negro woman that day when he was shooting at the Negro man."

Lion is the wild mongrel dog who is afraid of nothing. He is a mixture of many breeds, "part mastiff, something of airedale, and something of a dozen other strains probably." His color is frequently emphasized: "and all over that strange color like a blued gun-barrel." It is also the color of Boon's beard: "That blue stubble on his face like the filings from a new gun-barrel." The dog, too, is completely without sentiment. It appears only as a relentless force, without feeling, as for instance when it "hurled itself tirelessly against the door and dropped back and leaped again. It never made any sound and there was nothing frenzied in the act but only a cold and grim indomitable determination." This absence of feeling, of attachment, of "meanness or generosity or gentleness or viciousness," is replaced by a fixed purposefulness that is derived from nothing. It is merely a major element in the natural phenomenon which is the dog. There is only

> the blue hide beneath which the muscles flinched or quivered to no touch since the heart which drove blood to them loved no man and nothing, standing as a horse stands yet different from a horse which infers only weight and speed while Lion inferred not only courage and all else that went to make up the will and desire to pursue and kill, but endurance, the will and desire to endure *beyond all imaginable limits of flesh* in order to overtake and slay. (Italics are mine.)

It is not amiss here to note the similarity in some respects between Lion and Boon. Boon's eyes, too, are devoid of "meanness or generosity or gentleness or viciousness." Boon's beard is the same color as Lion's body, and Boon, in the course of the story, proves that he has limitless bravery. He finds himself drawn to Lion and becomes the servant of the dog.

> It was as if Lion were a woman—or perhaps Boon was the woman. That was more like it—the big, grave, sleepy-seeming dog which, as Sam Fathers said, cared about no man and no thing; and the violent, insensitive, hard-faced man with his touch of remote Indian blood and the mind almost of a child.

These are the similarities. A little later we will go into the differences.

In addition to Old Ben, Boon, and the dog, there are two other principal characters in this drama. Sam Fathers, like the bear, is an anachronism. He, too, is part of the wilderness, part of its very spirit and essence. He must live in it. He understands it, loves it, is bound by humility in the face of its natural wonders. Part Indian and part Negro, he combines the best of the innocence of both races. Civilization has not touched Sam Fathers. He is the human equivalent of Old Ben. His function in the story, as a figure representing the best of the past, is to be the finest possible teacher for Ike McCaslin.

When Ike is ten years old, he graduates from hunting rabbits and squirrels to hunting deer and bear. His entire tutelage is under Sam. Old Ben becomes for the boy the object of all hunting, the principal figure in the whole wilderness drama, which grows to be the dominant theme in his life: "It loomed and towered in his dreams before he ever saw the unaxed woods where it left its crooked print, shaggy, tremendous, red-eyed, not malevolent but just big." The boy dedicates himself to the woods, is baptized in blood as a hunter, and learns humility and "love and pity for all which lived and ran and then ceased to live in a second in the very midst of splendor and speed"; he even breaks the bonds of time and space to become part of the wilderness.

> He stood for a moment—a child, alien and lost in the green and soaring gloom of the markless wilderness. Then he re-linquished completely to it. It was the watch and the compass. He was still tainted. He removed the linked chain of the one and the looped thong of the other from his overalls and hung them on a bush and leaned the stick beside them and entered it.

## FINDING MEANING IN THE HUNTING STORY

These are the principal characters in "The Bear"; among them they provide its entire meaning. The meaning of the story is difficult to reach, yet the urge to examine it is compelling; as a hunting story it has little to do with hunting. Much space and time are devoted to minute descriptions of characters, who, except for Ike, never become real. They have no depth. They are clearly seen, but only for a moment. The bear is obviously no ordinary bear, just as the dog is no ordinary dog—they are forthright symbols. Since Old Ben is called "an anachronism, out of an old dead time," it does not require very much imagination to sense that in a way we have here a symbol, not only of the wilderness-past, the prehistoric past, but of all history, because the wilderness in its turn is merely a metaphor; it is whatever is past, all dead time. Therefore, an examination of how the bear is killed should reveal something of the nature of that progress which constitutes change. The death of the bear is a parable of mutation.

Two creatures, Lion and Boon, are responsible for Ben's death. Their relationship is important. Lion, as we have seen, is entirely without sentiment. He acts in relentless pursuit, never gives ground, is unresponsive to affection. He is, in fact, nothing recognizable at all, except that because of his function and with his gun-barrel-blue color and his brute strength, he seems to symbolize the undeviating force of destructive change. The mixture of breeds, mentioned before, further indicates the complexities and divisions of progress and makes more rigid the creature's allegorical nature, since it thus becomes less recognizable as a dog. It is mechanical in its characteristics, thus emphasizing the relentless, inevitable and automatic nature of change. The bear must die, the dog must kill—this is as much a part of the order of things as the rising and setting of the sun.

Boon requires more analysis, since he embodies a dichotomy. As we see most clearly from *A Fable*, Faulkner demands a positive morality, achieved by a conscious choice following an awareness of evil. There is nothing to evoke pride in the knowledge of innate innocence; it is the other kind of innocence consequent upon absolution from guilt that enables man to climb back into Eden. Boon never can make this ascent. He is immature man, a symbol for the infancy of both the individual and the race—Boon is part Indian and part white. The Indian part of him is presumably the primitive innocent. Within the figure of Boon, Faulkner has crystallized his view of the human plight. Boon, man, is a pathetic fallen Adam, unable, after the discovery of evil, to cope with and combat it and, therefore, unable to regain his former innocence. . . .

### IKE'S HUMAN QUALITIES

Into this story comes Ike, the specific human protagonist in the midst of the abstract allegory, who throughout is merely an observer, the student, trained by the pure man, Sam. Ike, being human, is not perfect; "only Sam and Old Ben and the mongrel Lion were taintless and incorruptible." Ike learns love and pity and pride and humility. Parentless, that is without a past directly forced upon him, he is able to stand back and observe objectively the values of past and present. Thus he does not kill the bear, but he is the only witness to its destruction. He has the opportunity to kill the bear but is outside the pageant of its demise. In the same way, it is he alone who is able to see Boon's final frustration with gun and squirrels. In the version we are discussing now, his visit to the gum tree is the last he will make to the wilderness. He goes there "one more time" to get one more lesson. He sees that it is Boon, so often mistaken as a noble participant in the drama, who has finally and completely introduced the concept of "mine" into the new world.

This is the story of the hunting of Old Ben and one way of looking at its meaning. It would appear that Ike is full of promise for redressing the wrongs resulting from the incompetence of such as Boon, since he is equipped with the best of the old values. . . .

Ike, [however,] represents Faulkner's point of view only in occasional sentences. The course which Ike follows in the novel is so drawn as to clearly indicate Faulkner's rejection of it. The course he should have followed is discoverable if one traces back the arguments of Ike and his cousin. There he reveals an awareness that he later betrays; he refuses to hold the land as God's overseer, even though he knows that this is required; he forsakes all obligation.

Ike was the first, and as far as we know, the only member of his family with moral awareness. Only he had Sam Fathers for father, who taught him the values which McCaslin, his cousin, reiterated: *"Courage and honor and pride, and pity and love of justice and of liberty. They all touch the heart, and what the heart holds to becomes truth, as far as we know truth."* Yet Ike, despite his moral equipment, remains socially ineffectual. He is unable to take part in human affairs, unable to do as Dilsey does in *The Sound and the Fury* or as the corporal does in *A Fable,* to apply his values to his circumstances, to operate in the real world with the knowledge of his heart. . . .

## FLAWS IN "THE BEAR"

We have writing here that veers toward allegory because the symbols do not suggest implications arising out of their very nature. Meanings are imposed by the author's intention. "The Bear" fails from its contrived nature. Its metaphors are not constructed out of the observable world of Faulkner's experience but are welded together artificially from Faulkner's intellect. The story is meaningless unless we understand the intended significance of the author's characters and events. Sam's death, for instance, is not explained away by the doctor's lecture on the power of mind over matter.

The critics can come to little agreement on the roles of Boon and Sam, and the bear itself has been called many things. But all critics are agreed that Faulkner had in mind a set of equivalents that are almost, if not quite, specific. Fiction must embody its point of view in a reality produced by the imagination. It is through the use of metaphor, image, and epithet that literature comes alive. The writer at his best sees his picture clearly, then makes us see what he sees, no less in prose than in poetry. Faulkner has let his point of view emerge here, not clearly, but sufficiently in his own mind to damage his attempt to write satisfactory fiction.

# "The Bear" as a Nature Myth

John Lydenberg

John Lydenberg analyzes William Faulkner's "The Bear," the long story from *Go Down, Moses,* as a nature myth, a magical tale in which humans must act in a world they neither understand nor control. Lydenberg identifies characters in the story as elements of traditional nature myths: Old Ben as a totem animal, a god; Sam Fathers as a priest; Ike as the young initiate; and the Jefferson hunters as the tribe. John Lydenberg, who has taught English at Hobart College in Geneva, New York, for many years, has published numerous critical articles in scholarly journals.

"The Bear" is by general agreement one of Faulkner's most exciting and rewarding stories. . . .

"The Bear," in its final version, can be summarized briefly. When Ike McCaslin is ten, he is first taken with a group of men on their yearly hunting trip into the wilderness of Sutpen's hundred. He quickly learns to be a good hunter under the tutelage of the old half-Indian, half-Negro guide, Sam Fathers. The routine hunting has an added goal: the killing of Old Ben, a huge and sage, almost legendary bear, who always defies capture. Sam Fathers maintains that none of their dogs can bring Old Ben to bay, and that they must find one stronger and braver. Finally he gets what he needs, a wild dog named Lion. When Ike is sixteen, the last chase occurs. Hunters shoot in vain, hounds are killed as they try to hold Ben. And then Lion rushes in, followed by Boon, the quarter-Indian retainer, who charges like the dog, directly upon the bear, to make the kill with his knife. Lion dies from his wounds the next day. Sam Fathers drops from exhaustion and dies shortly thereafter. The story proper is

Excerpted from "Nature Myth in Faulkner's 'The Bear'" by John Lydenberg, *American Literature*, vol. 24, no. 1 (March 1952), pp. 62–72. Copyright 1952, Duke University Press. Reprinted with permission.

then interrupted by Part IV, a section as long again as the rest. Part V is a short epilogue, telling of Ike's sole return to the scene of his apprenticeship, his visit to the graves of Lion and Sam Fathers, and his meeting with Boon.

On one level the story is a symbolic representation of man's relation to the land, and particularly the Southerner's conquest of his native land. In attempting to kill Old Ben, the men are contending with the wilderness itself. In one sense, as men, they have a perfect right to do this, as long as they act with dignity and propriety, maintaining their humility while they demonstrate the ability of human beings to master the brute forces of nature. The hunters from Jefferson are gentlemen and sportsmen, representing the ideals of the old order at its best, the honor, dignity, and courage of the South. In their rapport with nature and their contest with old Ben, they regain the purity they have lost in their workaday world, and abjure the petty conventions with which they ordinarily mar their lives. But as Southerners they are part of "that whole edifice intricate and complex and founded upon injustice"; they are part of that South that has bought and sold land and has held men as slaves. Their original sins have alienated them irrevocably from nature. Thus their conquest of Old Ben becomes a rape. What might in other circumstances have been right, is now a violation of the wilderness and the Southern land.

## PART IV AS SOCIAL COMMENTARY AND MYTH

Part IV makes explicit the social comment implied in the drama of Old Ben. It consists of a long and complicated account of the McCaslin family, white and mulatto, and a series of pronunciamentos by Ike upon the South, the land, truth, man's frailties and God's will. It is in effect Ike's spiritual autobiography given as explanation of his reasons for relinquishing and repudiating, for refusing to own land or participate actively in the life of the South. Ike discovers that he can do nothing to lift or lighten the curse the Southerners have brought on themselves, the monstrous offspring of their God-given free will. The price of purity, Ike finds, is noninvolvement, and he chooses purity.

Thus Part IV carries us far beyond the confines of the story of the hunt. It creates a McCaslin myth that fits into the broad saga of Faulkner's mythical kingdom, and it includes in nondramatic form a good deal of direct social comment.

The rest of "The Bear" cannot be regarded as *simply* a dramatic symbolization of Ike's conscientious repudiation. Its symbolism cannot fully be interpreted in terms of this social myth. One responds emotionally to the bear hunt as to a separate unit, an indivisible and self-sufficient whole. Part IV and Old Ben's story resemble the components of a binary star. They revolve about each other and even cast light upon each other. But each contains the source of its own light.

It is the mythical quality of the bear hunt proper that gives the story its haunting power. Beneath its other meanings and symbolisms lies the magical tale enacted by superhuman characters. Here religion and magic are combined in a ritual demonstration of the eternal struggle between Man and Nature. A statement of the legend recounting their partial reconciliation would run somewhat as follows:

Every fall members of the tribe make a pilgrimage to the domain of the Great Beast, the bear that is more than a bear, the preternatural animal that symbolizes for them their relation to Nature and thus to life. They maintain, of course, the forms of routine hunts. But beneath the conventional ritual lies the religious rite: the hunting of the tribal god, whom they dare not, and cannot, touch, but whom they are impelled to challenge. In this rite the established social relations dissolve; the artificial ranks of Jefferson give way to more natural relations as Sam Fathers is automatically given the lead. The bear and Sam are both taboo. Like a totem animal, Old Ben is at the same time sacred, and dangerous or forbidden (though in no sense unclean). Also he is truly animistic, possessing a soul of his own, initiating action, not inert like other creatures of nature. And Sam, the high priest, although alone admitted to the arcana[1] and trusted with the tutelage of the young neophyte, is yet outside the pale, living by himself, irrevocably differentiated from the others by his Negro blood, and yet kept pure and attuned to nature by his royal Indian blood.

### IKE'S INDUCTION INTO MANHOOD

This particular legend of man and the Nature God relates the induction of Ike, the natural and pure boy, into the mysteries of manhood. Guided by Sam Fathers, Ike learns how to retain his purity and bring himself into harmony with the

---

1. mysterious knowledge or language

forces of Nature. He learns human woodlore and the human codes and techniques of the hunt. And he learns their limitations. Old Ben, always concerned with the doings of his mortals, comes to gaze upon Ike as he stands alone and unprepared in a clearing. Ike "knew that the bear was looking at him. He never saw it. He did not know whether it was facing him from the cane or behind him." His apprehension does not depend on human senses. Awareness of his coming relation to the bear grows not from rational processes, but from intuition: "he knew now that he would never fire at it."

Yet he must see, must meet, Old Ben. He will be vouchsafed the vision, but only when he divests himself of manmade signs of fear and vanity. "*The gun,* the boy thought. *The*

---

### KILLING OLD BEN

*With a wild dog clutching his throat and a man mounted on his back stabbing him with a knife, Old Ben rises one last time, takes a few steps, and goes down like a felled tree.*

[Boon] could see Lion still clinging to the bear's throat and he saw the bear, half erect, strike one of the hounds with one paw and hurl it five or six feet and then, rising and rising as though it would never stop, stand erect again and begin to rake at Lion's belly with its forepaws. Then Boon was running. The boy saw the gleam of the blade in his hand and watched him leap among the hounds, hurdling them, kicking them aside as he ran, and fling himself astride the bear as he had hurled himself onto the mule, his legs locked around the bear's belly, his left arm under the bear's throat where Lion clung, and the glint of the knife as it rose and fell.

It fell just once. For an instant they almost resembled a piece of statuary: the clinging dog, the bear, the man stride its back, working and probing the buried blade. Then they went down, pulled over backward by Boon's weight, Boon underneath. It was the bear's back which reappeared first but at once Boon was astride it again. He had never released the knife and again the boy saw the almost infinitesimal movement of his arm and shoulder as he probed and sought; then the bear surged erect, raising with it the man and the dog too, and turned and still carrying the man and the dog it took two or three steps toward the woods on its hind feet as a man would have walked and crashed down. It didn't collapse, crumple. It fell all of a piece, as a tree falls, so that all three of them, man dog and bear, seemed to bounce once.

*gun.* 'You will have to choose,' Sam said." So one day, before light, he starts out unarmed on his pilgrimage, alone and helpless, with courage and humility, guided by his newly acquired woodlore, and by compass and watch, traveling till past noon, past the time at which he should have turned back to regain camp in safety. He has not yet found the bear. Then he realizes that divesting himself of the gun, necessary as that is, will not suffice if he wishes to come into the presence. "He stood for a moment—a child, alien and lost in the green and soaring gloom of the markless wilderness. Then he relinquished completely to it. It was the watch and the compass. He was still tainted."

He takes off the two artifacts, hangs them from a bush, and continues farther into the woods. Now he is at last pure—and lost. Then the footprints, huge, misshapen, and unmistakable, appear, one by one, leading him back to the spot he could no longer have found unaided, to the watch and the compass in the sunlight of the glade.

> Then he saw the bear. It did not emerge, appear; it was just there, immobile, fixed in the green and windless noon's hot dappling, not as big as he had dreamed it but as big as he had expected, bigger, dimensionless against the dappled obscurity, looking at him. Then it moved. It crossed the glade without haste, walking for an instant into the sun's full glare and out of it, and stopped again and looked back at him across one shoulder. Then it was gone. It didn't walk into the woods. It faded, sank back into the wilderness without motion as he had watched a fish, a huge old bass, sink back into the dark depths of its pool and vanish without even any movements of its fins.

## THE TRIBE AND ITS PRIEST, SAM FATHERS

Ike has seen the vision. That is his goal, but it is not the goal for the tribe, nor for Sam Fathers who as priest must prepare the kill for them. They are under a compulsion to carry out their annual ritual at the time of "the year's death," to strive to conquer the Nature God whose very presence challenges them and raises doubts as to their power.

The priest has first to make the proper medicine; he has to find the right dog. Out of the wilds it comes, as if sent by higher powers, untamable, silent, like no other dog. Then Sam, magician as well as priest, shapes him into the force, the instrument, that alone can master Old Ben. Lion is almost literally bewitched—broken maybe, but not tamed or civilized or "humanized." He is removed from the order of nature, but not allowed to partake of the order of civilization or humanity.

Sam Fathers fashions the instrument; that is his duty as it has been his duty to train the neophyte, to induct him into the mysteries, and thus to prepare, in effect, his own successor. But it is not for the priest to perform the impious and necessary deed. Because he belongs to the order of nature as well as of man—as Ike does now—neither of them can do more than assist at the rites. Nor can Major de Spain or General Compson or other human hunters pair with Lion. That is for Boon, who has never hit any animal bigger than a squirrel with his shotgun, who is like Lion in his imperturbable nonhumanity. Boon is part Indian; "he had neither profession job nor trade"; he has "the mind of a child, the heart of a horse, and little hard shoe-button eyes without depth or meanness or generosity or viciousness or gentleness or anything else." So he takes Lion into his bed, makes Lion a part of him. Divorced from nature and from man— "the big, grave, sleepy-seeming dog which, as Sam Fathers said, cared about no man and no thing; and the violent, insensitive, hard-faced man with his touch of remote Indian blood and the mind almost of a child"—the two mavericks live their own lives, dedicated and fated.

## THE FINAL HUNT

The "yearly pageant-rite" continues for six years. Then out of the swamps come the rest of the tribe, knowing the climax is approaching, accepted by the Jefferson aristocrats as proper participants in the final rites. Ike, the young priest, is given the post of honor on the one-eyed mule which alone among the mules and horses will not shy at the smell of blood. Beside him stands the dog who "loved no man and no thing." Lion "looked at him. It moved its head and looked at him across the trivial uproar of the hounds, out of the yellow eyes as depthless as Boon's, as free as Boon's of meanness or generosity or gentleness or viciousness. They were just cold and sleepy. Then it blinked, and he knew it was not looking at him and never had been, without even bothering to turn its head away."

The final hunt is short, for Old Ben can be downed only when his time has come, not by the contrived machinations of men, but by the destined ordering of events and his own free will. The hounds run the bear; a swamper fires; Walter

Ewell fires; Boon cannot fire. Then the bear turns and Lion drives in, is caught in the bear's two arms and falls with him. Ike draws back the hammers of his gun. And Boon, like Lion, drives in, jumps on Ben's back and thrusts his knife into the bear's throat. Again they fall. Then "the bear surged erect, raising with it the man and the dog too, and turned and still carrying the man and the dog it took two or three steps towards the woods on its hind feet as a man would have walked and crashed down. It didn't collapse, crumple. It fell all of a piece, as a tree falls, so that all three of them, man dog and bear, seemed to bounce once."

The tribe comes up, with wagon and mules, to carry back to camp the dead bear, Lion with his guts raked out, Boon bleeding, and Sam Fathers who dropped, unscathed but paralyzed, at the moment that Ben received his death wound. The doctor from the near-by sawmill pushes back Lion's entrails and sews him up. Sam lies quiet in his hut after talking in his old unknown tongue, and then pleading, "Let me out, master. Let me go home."

### AFTERMATH OF THE KILL

Next day the swampers and trappers gather again, sitting around Lion in the front yard, "talking quietly of hunting, of the game and the dogs which ran it, of hounds and bear and deer and men of yesterday vanished from the earth, while from time to time the great blue dog would open his eyes, not as if he were listening to them but as though to look at the woods for a moment before closing his eyes again, to remember the woods or to see that they were still there. He died at sundown." And in his hut Sam quietly goes after the bear whose death he was destined to prepare and upon whose life his own depended, leaving behind the de Spains and Compsons who will no longer hunt in this wilderness and the new priest who will keep himself pure to observe, always from the outside, the impious destruction of the remaining Nature by men who can no longer be taught the saving virtues of pride and humility. They have succeeded in doing what they felt they had to do, what they thought they wanted to do. But their act was essentially sacrilegious, however necessary and glorious it may have seemed. They have not gained the power and strength of their feared and reverenced god by conquering him. Indeed, as human beings will, they have mistaken their true relation to him. They tried to possess what they could not possess, and now they can no longer even share in it.

Boon remains, but he has violated the fundamental taboo. Permitted to do this by virtue of his nonhumanity, he is yet in part human. He has broken the law, killed with his own hand the bear, taken upon himself the mastery of that which was no man's to master. So when the chiefs withdraw, and the sawmills grind their way into the forests, Boon polices the new desecrations. When Ike returns to gaze once more upon the remnants of the wilderness, he finds Boon alone in the clearing where the squirrels can be trapped in the isolated tree. Boon, with the gun he could never aim successfully, frenziedly hammers the barrel against the breech of the dismembered weapon, shouting at the intruder, any intruder, "Get out of here! Don't touch them! Don't touch a one of them! They're mine!" Having killed the bear, he now possesses all the creatures of nature, and will snarl jealously at the innocent who walks peacefully through the woods. The result of his impiety is, literally, madness. . . .

## THE SIGNIFICANCE OF KILLING OLD BEN

Thus the killing of the bear cannot be explained by a naturalistic interpretation of the symbolism. Old Ben is not merely an extraordinary bear representing the wilderness and impervious to all but the most skillful or improper attacks. He is the totem animal, the god who can never be bested by men with their hounds and guns, but only by a nonhuman Boon with Lion, the instrument fashioned by the priest.

Sam Fathers' death can likewise be explained only by the nature myth. If the conquest of Old Ben is the triumphant culmination of the boy's induction into the hunting clan, Sam, his mentor, would presumably be allowed a share in the triumph. If the bear's death symbolizes the destruction of the wild, Sam's demise can be seen as paralleling that of the nature of which he is so completely a part. But then the whole affair would be immoral, and Sam could not manage and lead the case so willingly, nor would he die placid and satisfied. Only as part of a nature rite does his death become fully understandable. It is as if the priest and the god are possessed of the same soul. The priest fulfils his function; his magic makes the god vulnerable to the men. He has to do it; and according to human standards he wins a victory for his tribe. But it is a victory for which the only fit reward is the death he is content to accept. The actors act out their ordained roles. And in the end the deed brings neither jubilation nor mourning—only retribution, tragic in the high sense, right as the things which are inevitable are right.

A further paradox, a seeming contradiction, appears in the conjunction of the two words which are repeated so often that they clearly constitute a major theme. Pride and humility. Here conjoined are two apparently polar concepts: the quintessence of Christianity in the virtue of humility; and the greatest of sins, the sin of Satan. Though at first the words puzzle one, or else slip by as merely a pleasant conceit, they soon gather up into themselves the entire "meaning" of the story. This meaning can be read in purely naturalistic terms: Faulkner gives these two qualities as the huntsman's necessary virtues. But they take on additional connotations. Humility becomes the proper attitude to the nature gods, with whom man can merely bring himself into harmony as Sam teaches Ike to do. The pride arises out of the individual's realization of his manhood: his acquisition of the self-control which permits him to perform the rituals as he should. Actually it is humanly impossible to possess these two qualities fully at the same time. Sam alone truly has them, and as the priest he has partly escaped from his humanity. Ike apparently believes he has developed them, finally; and Faulkner seems to agree with him. But Ike cannot quite become Sam's successor, for in acquiring the necessary humility—and insight—he loses the ability to act with the full pride of a man, and can only be an onlooker, indeed in his later life, as told in Part IV and "Delta Autumn," a sort of Ishmael.[2]

In conclusion, then, "The Bear" is first of all a magnificent story. The inclusion of Part IV gives us specific insights into Faulkner's attitudes toward his Southern society and adds another legend to the saga of his mythical kingdom. The tale of Old Ben by itself has a different sort of effect. Our response is not intellectual but emotional. The relatively simple story of the hunting of a wise old bear suggests the mysteries of life, which we feel subconsciously and cannot consider in the rationalistic terms we use to analyze the "how" of ordinary life. Thus it appears as a nature myth, embodying the ambivalences that lie at the heart of primitive

2. an outcast and wanderer in the Old Testament

taboos, rituals, and religions, and the awe we feel toward that which we are unable to comprehend or master. From strata buried deep under our rationalistic understanding, it dredges up our feeling that the simple and the primitive— the stolid dignity and the superstitions of Sam Fathers—are the true. It evokes our terrible and fatal attraction toward the imperturbable, the powerful, the great—as symbolized in the immortal Old Ben. And it expresses our knowledge that as men we have to conquer and overcome, and our knowledge that it is beyond our human power to do so—that it is necessary and sacrilegious.

CHAPTER 3

# Faulkner's Major Works: 1929–1932

# Ambiguity in
# *The Sound and the Fury*

Walter J. Slatoff

In a conversational style, Walter J. Slatoff discusses the ambiguities in William Faulkner's *The Sound and the Fury* and concludes that Faulkner's characters evoke conflicting rather than clear impressions of who they are. In his search for the novel's organizing principles, Slatoff concludes that none of the possible motifs—old culture versus new, Christian symbolism, the character of Dilsey—emerges as a clear reference point. Consequently, Slatoff says, the novel seems to end where it began and leaves the reader with a sense of emotional and intellectual tension. Walter J. Slatoff has taught at Cornell University in New York and has published *With Respect to Readers; Dimensions of Literary Response* and *The Look of Distance; Reflections on Suffering and Sympathy in Modern Literature—Auden to Agee, Whitman to Woolf.*

*The Sound and the Fury* presents various parts of the history of the Compson family in four discontinuous sections, each of which is written from a different point of view and a different point in time. These temporal positions are not sequential; they run April 7, 1928; June 2, 1910; April 6, 1928; and April 8, 1928. In addition, within each of the first three sections there is a continual shuttling back and forth in time, ordered largely by the mental associations of the narrators, who are the idiot Benjy, the sensitive and romantic but neurotically obsessed Quentin, and the practical, materialistic, and self-pitying Jason. The first section is especially fragmented and difficult to embrace, since its narrator cannot distinguish time and has not developed with time, and shows his inability to understand any abstract relationships by omitting all connective tissue between his sentences.

As suggested above, this mode of presentation prevents us from organizing our impressions about any single center and induces a general sense of tension and disequilibrium.... We are not sure what attitude to take toward the disintegration of the family. In the first two sections, Benjy and Quentin report events in such a way that we see and feel their pathetic rather than ludicrous or ironic side. The "sassprilluh" drinking scene, for example, could easily have been presented with the same comic gusto we find in "The Spotted Horses." Instead the emphasis is upon Benjy's discomfort and upon the unhappy effect of T.P.'s laughter on Quentin. We are somewhat aware throughout the first two sections that Benjy is subhuman and that his suffering is not of an order that evokes the highest kind of sympathy, and Quentin's posturing and extreme romanticism at times seem comic, but essentially we are led to see them both as suffering individuals, to feel considerable compassion for them, and to take their predicaments very seriously. In the third section, however, narrated by Jason, the tone is essentially comic and satiric. Not only does Jason come through as a largely comic character but his narration tends to bathe the whole Compson history in a somewhat comic light, which at least temporarily blinds us to the poignancy and pathos of it. We are much more detached than in the earlier sections, less serious. We want to see Jason made a fool of, and we are not especially moved by the plight of his niece Quentin. Had the novel ended with this section we would view the Compson history largely with a sense of grim amusement, as a tale of sound and fury signifying that the human condition is essentially hopeless and not worth much thought or compassion.

Our response is further complicated by our conflicting feelings about most of the characters. We have sympathy for Benjy but can never forget that he is an idiot, who is oblivious to everyone's needs but his own, and that efforts to please or comfort him are in a sense futile. We can recognize that he is to some extent a measure or "moral mirror" for the other characters in that we can judge them in relation to their treatment of him and his response to them, but he is hardly an adequate measure since he is apparently as comforted by firelight or golfers as he is by Dilsey or Caddy. And if we admire Benjy's direct and uncomplicated responses to experience, his ability to sense evil, and his loyalty and see these as a celebration of primitivism on Faulkner's part, we must at the same time remember that Benjy is as much incapacitated as his mother or Quentin, or Emily Grierson for that matter, by his utter inability to let go of the past.

### LUSTER TORMENTS BENJY

*In* The Sound and the Fury, *Dilsey's son Luster makes Benjy frantic by driving the horse and wagon the "wrong" way around the monument. In this brief scene, Benjy bellows until Jason comes and turns the horse around.*

Luster hit Queenie again and swung her to the left at the monument.

For an instant Ben sat in an utter hiatus. Then he bellowed. Bellow on bellow, his voice mounted, with scarce interval for breath. There was more than astonishment in it, it was horror; shock; agony eyeless, tongueless; just sound. . . . With Ben's voice mounting toward its unbelievable crescendo Luster caught up the end of the reins and leaned forward as Jason came jumping across the square and onto the step.

With a backhanded blow he hurled Luster aside and caught the reins and sawed Queenie about and doubled the reins back and slashed her across the hips. He cut her again and again, into a plunging gallop, while Ben's hoarse agony roared about them, and swung her about to the right of the monument. Then he struck Luster over the head with his fist.

"Dont you know any better than to take him to the left?" he said. He reached back and struck Ben, breaking the flower stalk again. "Shut up!" he said, "Shut up!" He jerked Queenie back and jumped down. "Get to hell on home with him. If you ever cross that gate with him again, I'll kill you!"

"Yes, suh!" Luster said. He took the reins and hit Queenie with the end of them. "Git up! Git up, dar! Benjy, fer God's sake!"

Ben's voice roared and roared. Queenie moved again, her feet began to clop-clop steadily again, and at once Ben hushed. Luster looked quickly back over his shoulder, then he drove on. The broken flower drooped over Ben's fist and his eyes were empty and blue and serene again as cornice and façade flowed smoothly once more from left to right; post and tree, window and doorway, and signboard, each in its ordered place.

We admire Caddy for her devotion to Benjy but recognize that she is at the same time willful and domineering and does abandon Benjy. We are puzzled somewhat by her utter sense

of defeat after her affair with Dalton and by her willingness
to marry Herbert. This seems another example of a Faulkner
character acting in precisely the way which will lead to the
most self-torment. Nor are we ever really enlightened about
her character. We learn that she is concerned about her
daughter Quentin's welfare, but not concerned enough to do
anything serious about it. In the section narrated by Jason we
watch her suffer but gain little insight into why she behaves
as she does or how she feels beyond the moment.

We are likewise puzzled and confused by Quentin. We
sympathize with him but at the same time feel that he suffers
as much from a pathological condition which calls for psy-
chiatric care as from a tragic human dilemma which can
claim our entire compassion. We recognize the decency and
even nobility of many of his feelings but also a certain
amount of posturing, and we recognize that in his own way
he is as self-centered as Benjy. Finally, I think, we are mysti-
fied by him. I suppose no suicide is ever fully comprehensible to those who choose to live, but Quentin's is especially
difficult to understand. We know a great deal about his state
of mind after he has decided to die, and we know many of his
feelings about Caddy and her wedding, but we never see him
moving toward or reaching the decision to take his life. . . .

Even toward Jason we have conflicting feelings. In some
ways he is a monster, and in many ways he is a fool, and yet,
as Faulkner says in his Appendix, he is in some ways "the
first sane Compson since before Culloden." He is full of a
grandiose self-pity, but it is not entirely unwarranted, for
many a better man would consider himself cursed if he had
to cope with Mrs. Compson, Quentin II, and Benjy. Although
he fails utterly to recognize Dilsey's worth, his estimate of
the other Negroes is not entirely unjust. Luster, for example,
takes care of Benjy after a fashion but spends as much of his
time tormenting him as pacifying him. And if Jason is un-
justifiably cynical about all human actions, this permits him
to see through his mother in ways that we relish. Still further
complicating our response is the fact that he does in a sense
support the Compson family, that he does seem to make a
more satisfactory sexual adjustment than any of the other
Compson children, and that he has a sense of humor, albeit
a distorted and paranoiac one. Working most against any
resolution of feeling toward him are his violent headaches,
which compel a certain sympathy for him and which sug-

gest that he, too, is a suffering neurotic.

Dilsey and Mrs. Compson provide the least irresolution in our responses. We consistently admire Dilsey's decency, loyalty, and stoicism, and we disdain with equal consistency Mrs. Compson's foolishness and self-pity. Yet even these reactions are somewhat qualified, for Mrs. Compson is too silly to be seriously despised, and Dilsey spends much of her time nagging, scolding, and threatening both the Compson children and her own, and she is, in the last analysis, ineffectual.

## THE NOVEL LACKS A CLEAR ORGANIZING PATTERN

Besides being unsettled by these various and often conflicting feelings, we are groping at the end of the third section for some larger perspective, context, or pattern under which to view and interpret the unhappy events we have been witnessing. Faulkner has suggested a number of these. The title has suggested that there is no pattern, that the events have no significance, and Mr. Compson's nihilistic philosophy reinforces this, as does the apparently chaotic order of events. Opposed to this, however, is our natural disinclination to accept such a view, and our awareness of Faulkner's at least partial approval of Benjy, Quentin, Caddy, Mr. Compson, and Dilsey, and his disapproval of Mrs. Compson, Jason, and Herbert. There is also our recognition of several more or less recurrent motifs which encourage us to search for pattern and significance within and beneath the sound and fury. But the search has sent us in varying directions, none of which has been clearly or conclusively marked.

Some of the events and emphases have seemed chiefly in accord with a socioeconomic antithesis between an old and new culture. . . . Up to a point we can see in Mr. and Mrs. Compson, Quentin, and the Blands the remnants and corruptions of a traditional society which is in contrast with a rootless money-centered culture more or less typified by Jason, Luster, Herbert, and the carnival, with its performer on the musical saw and its dehumanized young man with the red tie, who runs away with Quentin II. To some extent one cannot avoid making some such schematization. On the other hand, there is much to keep one from being content with it. One cannot help feeling that most of the problems and difficulties of Benjy, Caddy, and Quentin are clinical rather than sociological; they seem driven more by peculiar personal need than by larger forces. . . .

To the extent that we do accept some such opposition between an older and newer order we are disturbed by the impossibility of choosing between them. Our sympathies, like Faulkner's, are with the old, but the best representatives of it in this book are a drunkard, a suicide, and a lost and lonely woman. Between what they are and what Jason is there seems no middle ground offered. Dilsey's decency suggests that there can be something better, but the kind of answer her presence implies is rather special and ambiguous and finally seems independent of a sociological schematization.

We have been encouraged, also, to seek patterns in several other directions. Some of the events and emphases have suggested interpretation in terms of clinical and even specifically Freudian psychology. We have been strongly encouraged, also, as various critics have pointed out, to interpret events in relation to Christian myth and ideology, in relation to concepts of time, and in relation to Shakespearian tragedy. As with the old-versus-new-order motif Faulkner has emphasized each of these aspects enough to tempt us to consider it as a possible framework for ordering the fragmented story, but he has not emphasized any one consistently or clearly enough for us to accept it as a center. We are unsettled, of course, not only by this intermittent quality of the individual motifs but by the number and variety of the possible interpretations we must hold in suspension.

## THE PRESENCE OF A CHRISTIAN MOTIF

The final section of the book, narrated from an omniscient and objective point of view, begins with a focus and emphasis that seem to offer a kind of implicit interpretation and resolution, one in accord with the sentiments and mood of Faulkner's Nobel Prize speech. The strong emphasis on Dilsey's fortitude, decency, and Christian humility and on her comprehensive view of time, as numerous critics have pointed out, provides a context for the unhappy events, a perspective from which to view them and a way to feel about them. On the other hand, this episode does not so much offer a synthesis or interpretation as a general vantage point and degree of moral affirmation. It does not help us to understand most of the particulars of the Compson story any better, to illuminate, say, the character and motives of Quentin and Caddy. Nor does it in any but a peripheral way relate to the socioeconomic context of the story. Although it asserts the relevance of Christianity to the story it does not really clarify the nature of that relevance nor make clear how seriously we are to take the Christian context. I think this occurs partly because Faulkner so strongly emphasizes the peculiarly Negro aspects of both the Easter service and Dilsey's responses and partly because the crucifixion-and-resurrection motif is such a general one. This motif can serve as an ironic or moral commentary on virtually any kind of evil or decadence and therefore does not especially illuminate the meaning of any particular variety. Furthermore, although there have been throughout the book recurrent allusions to the crucifixion and resurrection and recurrent symbolic suggestions of them, the actual difficulties of the Compsons have not been sufficiently presented in Christian terms to enable us to see how the Christian motif is really applicable to their predicament. Nor is there any clear connection in the episode between the emphasis on the crucifixion and resurrection and Dilsey's repeated choral commentary, "I seed de beginnin, en now I sees de endin." Nevertheless, whatever the episode leaves unclear or unresolved, its tone and general tenor do provide a general way of looking at and feeling about the story and a sense of resolution.

## DILSEY AS A POTENTIAL FOCAL POINT

But—and it is a very crucial "but," which most interpreters of the novel have ignored—the emphasis on Dilsey and her trip to church is at the beginning of the final section and is only one of several emphases in that section. It is followed by the lengthy description of Jason's vain and tormenting pursuit of Quentin, which provides a very different perspective, mood, and set of feelings. We are back in a realm of sound and fury, even of melodrama. We do not see Jason from the large perspective we have just shared with Dilsey, but respond to his frustration and defeat with a grim amusement and satisfaction only slightly leavened by pity. We cannot view his defeat as affirmative, for the "heroine" who has eluded him seems equally doomed. It is true that we might draw a sharp contrast between the ways Dilsey and Jason spend their Sunday and between Dilsey's sense of Christian acceptance and Jason's violent and impatient paranoia, and we might go on to contrast her slow and decorous walk to church with his frenzied dependence on the automobile, and these contrasts can be related to the general contrast between traditional and traditionless cultures. Here again, however, one cannot quite understand the relevance of the contrast except as generalized ironic commentary. Nor do we, I think, actually feel this contrast while reading this section. Essentially Dilsey and her church have receded into the landscape and seem barely relevant to Jason's predicament.

The final part of the last section emphasizes Benjy's misery and the callousness and swagger of Dilsey's grandson, Luster, as he torments Benjy, first by taking his bottle, then by shouting "Caddy," and finally by driving around the square in the wrong direction. We are reminded for a moment of Dilsey's decency and faith but only to feel its ineffectualness, for neither she nor the church service has touched Luster. The book closes with the carriage ride of Luster and Benjy—with our attention focused on a young Negro whose main desire is to show off and on an idiot, capable of serenity or anguish but little more than that. Faulkner emphasizes Benjy's terrible agony as Luster throws his world into disorder by going around the square in the wrong direction. Jason comes rushing across the square, turns the carriage around, and hits both Luster and Benjy. Benjy becomes serene again as the carriage moves in its usual direction and things flow by smoothly from left to right "each in its ordered place."

It is a powerful ending and a fitting one in its focus on Benjy and its application to the general theme of order and disorder running through the novel. But it is an ending which provides anything but a synthesis or resolution, and it leaves us with numerous conflicting feelings and ideas. We are momentarily relieved and pleased by the cessation of Benjy's suffering, but we are troubled by the fact that it has been achieved by Jason, who cares nothing for Benjy and is concerned only with maintaining an external and superficial decorum. We can hardly draw any real satisfaction from the serenity and order, because the serenity is the "empty" serenity of an idiot and the order is that demanded by an idiot. The general tenor of the episode is in accord with Mr. Compson's pessimism rather than Faulkner's Nobel Prize speech, for everything in it suggests the meaninglessness and futility of life.

This final scene does not negate the moderate affirmation of the Dilsey episode, nor does it really qualify it. Rather it stands in suspension with it as a commentary of equal force. We feel and are intended to feel, I think, that the events we have witnessed are at once tragic and futile, significant and meaningless. We cannot move beyond this. Nor does the final section help us to resolve whether the Compsons were defeated essentially by acts of choice or by a kind of doom, or whether the doom was chiefly a matter of fate or of psychological aberration or of socioeconomic forces. It is worth repeating that if we do accept as a primary motif the opposition between an older and newer culture we face the impossibility of choosing between them.

In short, the ending seems designed not to interpret or to integrate but to leave the various elements of the story in much the same suspension in which they were offered, and to leave the reader with a high degree of emotional and intellectual tension.

# Five Perspectives in *The Sound and the Fury*

Cleanth Brooks

Cleanth Brooks searches for a pattern, or order, in *The Sound and the Fury*. He approaches this task by analyzing each of the four major characters from five angles: the poetic style of each character's section, each character's capacity for love, time's meaning to each, eternity's meaning to each, and the relationship of each to the title, a quotation from Shakespeare's *Macbeth*. Cleanth Brooks was educated at Vanderbilt University in Tennessee and the University of Oxford in England and taught at Louisiana State University and Yale University. He is the author of numerous scholarly articles and *Modern Poetry and the Tradition, The Well-Wrought Urn,* and *The Hidden God.*

*The Sound and the Fury* proved to be Faulkner's first great novel, and in the opinion of many qualified judges it remains his best. . . . The salient technical feature of *The Sound and the Fury* is the use of four different points of view in the presentation of the breakup of the Compson family. This special technique was obviously of great personal consequence to Faulkner, as evidenced by his several references to it in the [early 1960s]. The story is told through one obsessed consciousness after another, as we pass from Benjy's near-mindlessness to the obsessed mind of Quentin and then to the very differently obsessed mind of Jason. The first three sections are all examples of the stream-of-consciousness method, and yet, as Lawrence Bowling has well observed, how different they are in movement, mood, and effect!

The reader's movement through the book is a progression from murkiness to increasing enlightenment, and this is natural, since we start with the mind of an idiot, go on next

Reprinted by permission of Louisiana State University Press from *William Faulkner: The Yoknapatawpha Country* by Cleanth Brooks. Copyright ©1963 by Yale University Press; LSU paperback edition, 1990.

through the memories and reveries of the Hamlet-like Quentin, and come finally to the observations of the brittle, would-be rationalist Jason. Part of the sense of enlightenment comes simply from the fact that we are traversing the same territory in circling movements, and the cumulative effect of names and characterizations begins to dramatize for us with compelling urgency a situation we have come to accept almost as our own.

Readers of this novel some thirty years ago were shocked at what seemed an almost willful obscurity, and the difficulties entailed by Faulkner's method are not to be minimized. Some passages in Quentin's section, for example, seem to me so private as to be almost incomprehensible. But a generation of sensitive readers has testified to the almost palpable atmosphere of the first sections of the book. We do learn what it is like to live in such a family through being forced to share the minds of the three brothers in their special kinds of obsession. The sense of frustration and "entrapment" is overpowering. Benjy is obviously a victim in the sense in which an animal is, but Quentin is hardly less so, and even the horribly "sane" Jason feels victimized, as he shows in his compulsive talk. There is, therefore, as we move toward the end of the book, the sense of coming out into an objective world, a world in which objects take on firmness of outline and density and weight, in which objective truth, and not mere obsessional impressions, exists. Though the fourth section is not passed through Dilsey's mind, it is dominated by Dilsey; and the world in which Dilsey moves is an objective world, not simply the projection of a distempered spirit.

## THE PERSPECTIVE OF POETRY

The states of consciousness of the three brothers provide three quite different modes of interpretation. Consider them, for a moment, under the rubric of poetry. Benjy's section is filled with a kind of primitive poetry, a poetry of the senses, rendered with great immediacy, in which the world—for Benjy a kind of confused, blooming buzz—registers with great sensory impact but with minimal intelligibility. Quentin's section is filled with poetry too, though his is essentially decadent: sensitive but neurotic and hopeless, as it rings sadly through a series of dying falls. Entering Jason's section, we have no poetry at all, since Jason, the "sane" man, has consciously purged his mind of every trace of this perilous and impractical stuff. (One might claim, to be sure, that Jason's section does in fact attain to poetry, since perfect expression is in itself a kind of poetry. Jason's brilliant, if unconscious, parade of his vulgarity and his relentless exposure of his essential viciousness do carry prose—though ordinary and unpretentious—to the very brink of poetry.) With the last section we again encounter poetry, but of a more usual kind, especially in those passages which reveal Dilsey's reaction to the Easter service; and here it is neither primitive nor decadent, but whole, complex, and mature.

## THE PERSPECTIVE OF LOVE

We can look at the four sections in quite another way, noticing what different conceptions of love they imply. Benjy represents love in its most simple and childlike form. His love for Caddy is intense and unreflective. To him Caddy smells like trees. The syllables of her name—when he hears the golfers call out *caddy*—cause him to break out into hopeless crying, but his love is necessarily inarticulate and therefore almost formless.

Quentin's love for Caddy is self-conscious, formal, even abstract. Quentin believes that he is so much in love with his sister that he would gladly die in order to pull her away from the noise of the loud world and find in some corner of hell a quiet refuge for himself and her. He begs his father to believe that they have committed incest; but Quentin is not really in love with his sister's body, only in love with a notion of virginity that he associates with her. Though he thinks he is committing suicide because Caddy has given herself to various men and then has been forced into a loveless marriage, Quentin is really, as his sister knows, in love with death itself.

In contrast with this incestuously Platonic lover, Jason has no love for Caddy at all, and no love for anyone else. His notion of the proper amatory relationship is to provide himself with a "good honest whore." The relationship he desires is a commercial one: you know where you stand; there is no romantic nonsense about it. Jason, if he could, would reduce all relationships to commercial transactions.

## THE PERSPECTIVE OF TIME

Another way in which to contrast the first three sections is to observe the different notions of time held by the Compson brothers. Critic Perrin Lowrey finds that each of the brothers has a defective sense of time. Benjy, of course, is unconscious of time. Past and present jumble together in his mind, and so in the first section of the book the reader moves from one event to another, sometimes, without warning, across a gap of years, since for Benjy events are related only through some casual and accidental association. In contrast, Quentin is obsessed with time. In the long stream-of-consciousness meditation which occupies his section of the book, his obsession comes out in dozens of ways, including his avoidance of looking at clocks. Jason, too, is harried by time, but in a very different way: far from wishing to obliterate it, he would like to catch up with it. Throughout his section Jason is always racing the clock and is usually late because he always thinks of time, as Lowrey says, in a "mechanical and minute-to-minute sense." It is only in the fourth section of the book, the one dominated by Dilsey, that we enter into a proper notion of time. Dilsey knows how to interpret her backward and defective kitchen clock. When it strikes five times she automatically corrects the error and announces that it is eight o'clock. Her ability to make sense of the clock is simply one aspect of her ability to make sense of past, present, and future. All are aspects of eternity, and Dilsey, in her simple religious faith, believes in an order that is grounded in eternity.

Jean-Paul Sartre[1] has argued, in an essay that has proved most influential, that Faulkner's characters, because they are committed to the past, are helpless. The Faulknerian character's point of view, as Sartre described it in a graphic metaphor, is that of a passenger looking backward from a speeding car, who sees, flowing away from him, the landscape he is traversing. For him the future is not in view, the present is too blurred to make out, and he can see clearly only the past as it streams away before his obsessed and backward-looking gaze. . . . Perhaps a more accurate way of stating the truth that inheres in Sartre's view is to say: man's very freedom is bound up with his sense of having some kind of future. Unless he can look ahead to the future, he is not free. The relation that the three Compson brothers bear to the future and to time in general has everything to do, therefore, with their status as human beings.

1. French writer and philosopher

Benjy, as we have seen, is locked almost completely into a timeless present. He has not much more sense of time than an animal has, and therefore he possesses not much more freedom than an animal does. . . . A human being, of course, can project himself into the future not for hours or weeks but for years and decades.

---

**DILSEY'S EASTER SUNDAY**

*In the last section of* The Sound and the Fury, *Dilsey takes Benjy and Luster to church where the preacher delivers a long, inspiring sermon. The excerpt gives the minister's last words and Dilsey's response; it also shows that Dilsey has a sense of time and eternity.*

Whut I see? Whut I see, O sinner? I sees de resurrection en de light; sees de meek Jesus sayin Dey kilt Me dat ye shall live again; I died dat dem whut sees en believes shall never die. Breddren, O breddren! I sees de doom crack en hears de golden horns shoutin down de glory, en de arisen dead whut got de blood en de ricklickshun[1] of de Lamb!"

In the midst of the voices and the hands Ben sat, rapt in his sweet blue gaze. Dilsey sat bolt upright beside, crying rigidly and quietly in the annealment and the blood of the remembered Lamb.

As they walked through the bright noon, up the sandy road with the dispersing congregation talking easily again group to group, she continued to weep, unmindful of the talk.

"He sho a preacher, mon He didn't look like much at first, but hush!"

"He seed de power en de glory."

"Yes, suh. He seed hit. Face to face he seed hit."

Dilsey made no sound, her face did not quiver as the tears took their sunken and devious courses, walking with her head up, making no effort to dry them away even. . . .

"I've seed de first en de last," Dilsey said. "Never you mind me."

"First en last whut?" Frony said.

"Never you mind," Dilsey said. " I seed de beginnin, en now I sees de endin."

1. recollection

---

Quentin's obsession with the past is in fact a repudiation of the future. . . . Caddy's betrayal of her honor and the fact that she is cut off forever from Quentin mean that he pos-

sesses no future he is willing to contemplate. Thus, with relation to the future—any future—Quentin is listless and apathetic. He would like to do away with time, locking himself
into some past from which there would be no development
and no progression. Hence the dream that appeals to
Quentin: time congealed into a changeless moment; he and
Caddy in some cozy private niche in hell, enclosed in the
clean flame, isolated from everything else. Quentin's wish to
do away with time finds a symbolic expression in his twist-
ing the hands from his watch. . . .

As for the remaining Compson brother, if the lack of a future entails a lack of freedom for both Benjy, who is little
more than an animal, and for Quentin, who cannot look at
the future, Jason at least, with his rejection of the past and
his constant gaze into the future, ought, one might suppose,
to have complete freedom. But Jason, by insisting on seeing
time only with regard to something to be done, is incapable
of any real living. Like the frenetic businessman, Jason is always preparing to live, not living. . . . Jason is so committed
to preparation for the future that he is almost as enslaved as
are his brothers.

### THE PERSPECTIVE OF ETERNITY

I have said that to Dilsey neither the past nor the future nor
the present is oppressive, because to her they are all aspects
of eternity, and her ultimate commitment is to eternity. It
may be useful therefore to notice how the plight of each of
the brothers constitutes a false interpretation of eternity.
Benjy lives in a specious eternity: his present does not include all in timelessness—past, present, and future gathered
together in a total pattern—but is a purely negative eternity,
since it contains no past and no future. Quentin, we may say,
wants to take eternity by storm—to reach it by a sort of
shortcut, which in effect means freezing into permanence
one fleeting moment of the past. Eternity is thus for Quentin
not something which fulfills and enfolds all time, but simply
a particular segment of time, like one note of music infi-
nitely sustained. Jason is committed neither to a timeless
present nor to a frozen past but to a making ready for the
truly happy state. Jason's eternity is the empty mirage of an
oasis toward which he is constantly flogging his tired camel
and his tired self.

Though these patternings do emerge from a contemplation of the first three sections, and though they are important for an understanding of the novel, they do not show on the surface. The reader's impression of *The Sound and the Fury* is not of an elaborately formal abstract structure but quite the reverse. Rarely has a novel appeared so completely disordered and unconnected and accidental in its concreteness. Benjy's section has notoriously seemed a clutter of facts and memories, hard particularities and irrational concretions, a cluster that illustrates nothing and points nowhere. Quentin's section is only less difficult than Benjy's, though certainly quite as rich in conveying the sounds, smells, and shapes of a particular world. It is the apparent formlessness of so much of the book that has tempted the commentators to insist upon the underlying patterns. . . .

## DILSEY AS A SYMBOL OF UNITY AND MEANING

The one member of the Compson household who represents a unifying and sustaining force is the Negro servant Dilsey. She tries to take care of Benjy and to give the girl Quentin the mothering she needs. In contrast to Mrs. Compson's vanity and whining self-pity, Dilsey exhibits charity and rugged good sense. . . . Her view of the world and mankind is thoroughly Christian, simple and limited as her theological expression of her faith would have to be. On the other hand, Dilsey is no plaster saint. She is not easy on her own children. ("Dont stand dar in de rain, fool," she tells Luster.) She does not always offer the soft answer that turneth away wrath. . . . Dilsey's goodness is no mere goodness by, and of, nature, if one means by this a goodness that justifies a faith in man as man. Dilsey does not believe in man; she believes in God. . . .

The first three sections of the book do little to carry forward the story of what happened at the Compsons' on the Easter weekend. . . . Easter Sunday breaks bleak and chill and gray. It begins appropriately with Mrs. Compson's complaining and Dilsey's getting the fire started and the household tasks going, but once it is discovered that Quentin is not in her room, events accelerate. All of Jason's frenetic activity comes to a head when he makes the horrified discovery that his victim has found out where he has hidden the money that he has stolen from her and has escaped with it. But we do not immediately follow Jason on his frantic pursuit of his niece. Instead, once Jason is out of the house on his way to the sheriff's, we follow Dilsey and Benjy to church for the Easter service, and this service, in which Dilsey finds her exaltation, is counterpointed against Jason's attempt to find his niece and retrieve the money. . . . Easter morning brings to Dilsey a vision that gives meaning to human events. . . .

## THE SIGNIFICANCE OF THE TITLE

Faulkner's titles are often whimsical, containing some meaning private to himself which never becomes completely clear in the novel. The title of *The Sound and the Fury,* however, provides a true key, for the novel has to do with the discovery that life has no meaning. Shakespeare's lines from *Macbeth,* "[Life] is a tale/Told by an idiot, full of sound and fury,/Signifying nothing," quite aptly apply to the first section of the novel. Benjy's section, a tale told by an idiot, is not a tale told at all, but a kind of fuguelike arrangement and rearrangement of sights, smells, sounds, and actions, many of them meaningless in themselves, but tied together by some crisscross of association.

Quentin's section, too, echoes the title. Quentin has learned all too well his father's despairing philosophy, which sees human beings as merely dolls filled with sawdust. What spills from the side of such a doll can never be the healing blood of a Savior, with its promise of redemption. Quentin's own phrasing is: "dolls stuffed with sawdust swept up from the trash heaps where all previous dolls had been thrown away the sawdust flowing from what wound in what side that not for me died not."

Jason hopes to find meaning in life by discarding all idealisms, illusions, and emotional ties, and reducing life to its inexorable brass tacks. He manages to come out with a meaning of a sort, but it is a very thin and impoverished one. At the end of the novel he has scarcely made good his boast that he is a free man able to stand on his own feet with no help from anybody. He has indeed finally succeeded, with his brittle rationalism, in outsmarting himself.

For Dilsey life does have meaning, though many of her betters would dismiss what she takes to be its meaning as illusion, the opium dispensed to a poor and illiterate people. Faulkner makes no claim for Dilsey's version of Christianity one way or the other. His presentation of it is moving and credible, but moving and credible as an aspect of Dilsey's own mental and emotional life. At any rate, it does not avail for those who will not avail themselves of it. Mrs. Compson is much too tightly locked up in her own egotism and self-pity to derive any help from it, and Jason has consciously disavowed it long ago.

Faulkner closes his novel with a final confrontation of the two remaining Compson brothers, the one who believes he can live by pure reason alone and the other who is bereft of reason, neither of whom is, therefore, fully human. Meaning for Benjy is succession in due order, driving around the courthouse square to the right of the monument rather than the left. When Luster, bored and mischievous, whips up the mare and swings her to the left of the monument, Benjy finds himself confronted by nightmare and screams his outrage—the store fronts and buildings of Jefferson are all moving in insane reverse from the order in which he knows he ought to find them. Hearing Benjy's outcry, the maddened Jason, now back from the fruitless chase after his niece, snatches the reins and, cursing, turns the old horse into the accustomed route. Whereupon Benjy ceases his bellowing as his world moves again into accustomed order, "as cornice and façade flowed smoothly once more from left to right; post and tree, window and doorway, and signboard, each in its ordered place." This is about as much meaning as experience can have for Benjy. For his frenzied "sane" brother, experience has hardly this much.

# How *As I Lay Dying* Came to Be

Joseph Blotner

Joseph Blotner says that William Faulkner wrote
*As I Lay Dying* in forty-seven days while working
full-time shoveling coal because the entire novel
had taken shape in his mind from the start. Blotner
explains that though it builds on previous work, the
novel introduces a new family, the Bundrens and
their five children, and names Faulkner's Yoknapatawpha County for the first time. Told by fifteen
characters in a series of interior monologues,
*As I Lay Dying* centers around the death of Addie
Bundren, the mother, and the family's journey to
Jefferson to bury her. Joseph Blotner has written
a two-volume biography of William Faulkner. In
addition, he is the author of *The Modern American
Political Novel: 1900–1960* and the editor of books
containing Faulkner's letters and stories.

When Faulkner planned to work away from his home work-
room, he would roll up the segment he had begun, together
with an ample supply of blank sheets, secure the roll with a
sturdy elastic band, and put it in his pocket. On October 25,
1929, the day after panic had broken out on Wall Street, he
took one of these sheets and wrote at the top in blue ink "As
I Lay Dying." Then he underlined it twice and wrote the date
in the upper right-hand corner.

The two-story thirty-year-old powerhouse of brick squat-
ted beside the tall smokestack that rose above it. Inside,
wrote one historian, the "electric generator symbolized the
University's entrance into the technological age of the twentieth century." The building compactly housed the furnaces,
boilers, the huge wheel and belt, the pulley and dynamo,
and the banks of equipment with their gauges and switches.

Faulkner would later describe his laborious job. "I shoveled coal from the bunker into a wheelbarrow and wheeled it and dumped it where the fireman could put it into the boiler. About 11 o'clock the people would be going to bed, and so it did not take so much steam. Then we could rest, the fireman and I. He would sit in a chair and doze. I had invented a table out of a wheelbarrow in the coal bunker, just beyond a wall from where a dynamo ran. It made a deep, constant humming noise. There was no more work to do until about 4 A.M., when we would have to clean the fires and get up steam again." This gave him enough time each night, he later said, so that he "could write another chapter by about 4 A.M.". . .

In writing *As I Lay Dying,* he felt none of the rapture he had experienced with *The Sound and the Fury.* Like *Sanctuary,* this was a "deliberate" book. "I set out deliberately to write a tour-de-force.[1] Before I ever put pen to paper and set down the first word I knew what the last word would be. . . . Before I began I said, I am going to write a book by which, at a pinch, I can stand or fall if I never touch ink again." A year and a half before, sitting down each morning to *The Sound and the Fury,* he had felt a combination of faith and expectation and even ecstasy. "It was not there in As I Lay Dying. I said, It is because I knew too much about this book before I began to write it." He had already used the title twice before for versions of the spotted-horses episode from *Father Abraham.* When asked about it, he would sometimes recite a line—"As I lay dying the woman with the dog's eyes would not close my eyelids for me as I descended into Hades." It was the speech of ghostly Agamemnon to Odysseus in the Eleventh Book of the *Odyssey.*

## *AS I LAY DYING* STRUCTURED AROUND A NEW FAMILY

What Faulkner was doing night after night as he wrote to the hum of the powerhouse dynamo was to structure his novel around a family which had not appeared in *Father Abraham.* Anse and Addie Bundren had five children, the youngest of them—a girl and a small boy—sleeping together as Jo-Addie and Elmer Hodge had done in *Elmer.* Besides Henry Armstid, there were others from *Father Abraham:* Vernon Turpin, Will Varner, one of the Littlejohn family, and even one spotted horse (a descendant of the original herd,

1. a challenging task requiring great strength, often undertaken for its difficulty

since the time was twenty-five years later), ridden by Jewel Bundren. There were numerous other echoes—phrases and even whole scenes—from the two earlier works. The idea from which the whole book grew, Allen Tate[2] would remember Faulkner saying, was Anse Bundren's reflection that his troubles had come with the building of the road, that once it was built, it was easy for bad luck to find him. Young Vardaman Bundren might not have been too different from young Admiral Dewey Snopes if it had not been for the imminent traumatic loss of his dying mother, Addie. Faulkner had depicted sultry nubile country girls before, but in Dewey Dell Bundren he would outdo himself. If Cash, the quiet eldest son, was a recognizable country type, Darl at first glance might seem unfamiliar and utterly different from the other Bundrens. Actually, he was another representative of a type which had always fascinated Faulkner: the madman with poetic gifts.

As he later said, "I took this family and subjected them to the two greatest catastrophes which man can suffer—flood and fire, that's all. . . . That was written in six weeks without changing a word because I knew from the first where that was going." In the first story, the disaster had sprung from duplicity, greed, and naïveté. Now, though obligation to the dead would be the ostensible motive, it was shiftless Anse's desire for false teeth and a new wife that would subject Addie's children and her own putrefying body to the twin catastrophes. Faulkner was still dealing with some of the same constants: the evil and folly of men, a spectacle mitigated only by indignation, compassion, and humor.

His title was now more closely linked to the story than it had been when he used it in the version of elements from *Father Abraham*. It was a woman now, rather than a man, stretched out supine as in death, but as Clytemnestra had betrayed her husband Agamemnon with Aegisthus, so Addie had betrayed Anse with the Reverend Whitfield, the father of Jewel. But her major aspect was that of a victim—dying on a corn-shuck mattress while her husband looked toward her burial.

The manuscript pages accumulating under the minuscule strokes of his pen made it clear that Faulkner did know exactly where he was going. There were far fewer canceled

2. American author and critic

passages, marginal inserts, and paste-ins than in the manuscripts of his other novels. He may well have been using material from the lost 203 pages—whatever they were—that
had preceded the seventeen-page version of the story he had
called "As I Lay Dying." Here the dialect was not oppressively
heavy, as it had been in that story, though the novel also employed an experimental style. He was using the stream-of-
consciousness technique, though sparingly, and even when
he used it for Darl, it was never as hard to follow as it had
been with Benjy and Quentin.[3] There would be a total of fifteen characters, whose fifty-nine interior monologues, varying from one line to several pages, were most often more like
soliloquies or the direct address of Jason Compson than the
flowing and shifting memories and meditations of Quentin.
But as the narrators of that novel had turned toward a central female figure, Caddie, who had no segment of her own,
so more than one of these characters Faulkner was creating
was preoccupied with another female figure, dying Addie,
who was given only one narrative segment. . . .

Early in *As I Lay Dying* a familiar motif in Faulkner's work
appeared, an abnormal bond between a sister and brother,
though it would be far from incestuous. As early as page 11
of the manuscript, Dewey Dell thought of the knowledge of
Addie's death which Darl had telepathically shared with her.
Another paragraph, full of curiously fetal imagery, revealed
his knowledge that she was pregnant by her lover, Lafe. . . .
Darl's clairvoyance was clear. She would feel his eyes on her
during the funeral trip to come, knowing not only her
predicament but also, presumably, that her own ulterior motive for the trip was an abortion. Instead of the mutual empa-
thy conveyed in the canceled passages, however, her feeling
for her brother would change to destructive hostility.

### FAULKNER USED CHARACTERS FROM EARLIER WORKS

Though Faulkner's principal characters were new, he
reached back into what he called his lumber-room for others who not only served present purposes but also provided
links to other work. "I found out," he later said, "that not
only each book had to have a design but the whole output or
sum of an artist's work had to have a design." One such link-
ing character was Doc Peabody, from *Sartoris.* Seventy years

3. in *The Sound and the Fury*

old, weighing over two hundred pounds, he sees himself "hauled up and down a damn mountain on a rope," summoned by so inept a husband that he knows the wife must already be beyond his help. Like Shrevlin McCannon in his involvement with Quentin Compson, Peabody, with his combination of practicality and wisdom, would provide a counterweight to the tragic and bizarre elements in the Bundrens' recitals.

He was striving for a wide range of effects in these interior monologues. In some, such as those of Cora and Vernon Tull (changed from Turpin), the voices were authentic over their whole wide range of moods and tones. In others he imposed a convention upon the reader: a kind of poetic license whereby a character's thoughts would be rendered in language far beyond his capabilities—as he had done years before in the sketch "The Longshoreman." This was especially true of Darl, but it was also true of the child Vardaman, who could say of Jewel's horse, "I see him dissolve—legs, a rolling eye, a gaudy splotching like cold flames—and float upon the dark in fading solution. . . ." But when they speak aloud, all of their speech is faithful to their class. In Darl's first soliloquy, he had begun "Father and I," but Faulkner changed it to "Pa and Vernon Tull." The first would have been right for Quentin Compson, but it was not right for Darl Bundren.

## FAULKNER NAMES HIS COUNTY "YOKNAPATAWPHA"

Addie Bundren dies at that Faulknerian time of day: twilight. Cash, the good carpenter, makes her coffin himself, completing the work in the downpour which creates the flood. It makes their route so circuitous that they even leave the county. "They came from some place out in Yoknapatawpha county," one man says, "trying to get to Jefferson with it." In this narrative Faulkner had named his county.

He later said, "It's a Chickasaw Indian word meaning water runs slow through flat land." It appeared on old maps, transliterated as Yockeney-Patafa, to be shortened in modern times to Yocona, the name the river now bore. According to one scholar, a native of Oxford, Faulkner "normally accepts the physical facts of Oxford and of Lafayette County as coinciding with those of his Jefferson and Yoknapatawpha County." He would use many clearly identifiable places and geographical features, changing their names and usually altering their features. Eventually he called it his "apocryphal county," and it took on symbolic qualities which permitted it to stand for much more than Lafayette County or any other "real" one could. It was through this countryside that the forty-mile journey lay toward Addie's family burying ground, the pathetic cortege soon followed by buzzards drawn by the corpse putrefying in the July heat.

Like most of the women in the novel, Cora Tull is incensed at these outrages visited on Addie's body, feeling them symbolic of the hard lot of a hill farmer's wife. When Vernon tells her that it was a log which upset the wagon in the river, Cora replies, "Log, fiddlesticks. It was the hand of God." It may have been with this line in mind that Faulkner added a marginal insert to the preceding passage in which Darl described the actual event: *"It surged up out of the water and stood for an instant upright upon that surging and heaving desolation like Christ."* In revising the Benjy section of *The Sound and the Fury,* Faulkner had added overt Christian references. Now, however, just before the catastrophc of fire was to be visited upon the Bundrens, Faulkner deleted a passage heavy with Christian references. It was a portion of Darl's interior monologue in which he decided to set fire to Gillespie's barn to dispose of the rotting body: "Once when I was dead I heard the sad horns. I heard the sad suspirant they call Christ when the earth turned in slumber and slept again. . . . Once I was a little Child and I set up in dying. My father set me up in dying. It was a good business but I just wasn't the man for it. I hadn't the aptitude for it. For not all men are born carpenters, good carpenters, like Christ." The deletion preserved the suspense about the cause of the fire and also worked as the other deletions had done: to reduce the irrational element in the interior monologues of the Bundren family.

## THE JOURNEY COMPLETED

Between the catastrophes of flood and fire, Faulkner placed the monologue of Addie Bundren. Flanked by the monologues of the garrulous, obtuse, and self-righteous Cora Tull and the sanctimonious Reverend Whitfield, Addie's words convey her deep sense of alienation and bitterness. They also reveal a source of tragedy like that of the Compsons: a father whose counsel was one of utter despair, who had told her "the reason for living is getting ready to stay dead."

The trip to bury her (with borrowed shovels) in the family plot has proved a costly one, with the mules drowned in the river and Jewel's horse traded away to replace them. Dewey Dell has failed to obtain an abortion and Vardaman's emotional trauma has deepened. Cash's broken leg, sustained in the river disaster, has made him a cripple for life, and Darl, revealed as the arsonist, has been taken off to the state asylum. But Jewel has saved Addie from flood and fire, as she had predicted. And not only has Anse kept his promise to her, he has gained his ulterior objects: false teeth and a wife to replace her.

Faulkner completed the final five pages of the manuscript with no marginal inserts and only two passages from earlier sheets pasted onto the last page. Then he wrote at the bottom of page 107 "Oxford, Miss./11 December, 1929." Forty-seven days had elapsed since he had started. Typing it out, he did far less revision than he had with the earlier books. Though there were dozens of corrections in all, they were essentially minor. On January 12, 1930, it was completed. He sent off the original to Hal Smith, to whom he would dedicate the book. Then he bound the carbon copy with cardboard and mottled paper of blue, green, and cream nebulae and put it on his shelf.

# The Old Testament Themes in *As I Lay Dying*

Philip C. Rule

Philip C. Rule argues that William Faulkner's *As I Lay Dying* reflects Old Testament language and themes. Rule draws parallels between events in the novel and the wandering tribes of Israel and the life of Job. He quotes Psalms to show similarities in language, rhythm, and ideas and elaborates the biblical concepts of solidarity and alienation as they are reflected in *As I Lay Dying*. Philip C. Rule has taught English at the University of Detroit and served as literary editor of the journal *America*.

In searching out the religious values that underlie *As I Lay Dying*, critics have suggested Greek and Roman influences, Calvinism, and the Christian message in general. However, nothing so permeates the tone and texture of the story as does the spirit of the Old Testament. The themes, the attitudes, and frequently the very words and prose rhythms derive from the written account of the "pre-Christian" experience. Specifically, the story as a whole has strong overtones of the Book of Job. Salvation, religiosity, tribal solidarity, the importance of sex as an almost religious act—these and other Old Testament themes assert themselves. Where we might also expect a patriarchal society, Faulkner with typical irony gives us a matriarchal one. Above all, there is the brooding Old Testament spirit of despair, hope, endurance— tensions as old as mankind—with which man faces the darkness and mystery of the world around him.

The plot is deceptively simple: A woman dies and her family fulfills its promise to take her body back to her own family burial ground. At the outset we are reminded of the patriarch Jacob's charge to his sons: "I am to be gathered to

From Philip C. Rule, "The Old Testament Vision in *As I Lay Dying* , in *Religious Perspectives in Faulkner's Fiction: Yoknapatawpha and Beyond*, edited by J. Robert Barth, S.J. ©1972 by the University of Notre Dame Press. Used by permission.

my people: bury me with my fathers in the cave that is in the field of Ephron the Hittite" (Genesis, 49:29). And as, no doubt, the patriarch's sons could handle personal errands while carrying out this sacred obligation, we find the Bundrens capitalizing on the lugubrious trip to Jefferson: Dewey Dell to seek an abortion; Cash to buy a graphophone; Anse to get a new set of teeth—and a new wife. Those familiar with the Old Testament know that its characters were quite capable of very human motivation. . . .

The book is in fact a poetic meditation on the mysteries to which the human mind inevitably turns. Life and death, success and failure, loneliness and solidarity confront us in rhythmic patterns. Here we find the bitter-sweet of human life, in which the dignity of man is asserted only to be overshadowed by the awe-inspiring immensity of the Infinite. Faulkner's world is a grim demanding valley of tears where the struggle to eke out an existence from the soil is seen as [he said in "The Bear,"] "man's puny gnawing at the immemorial flank."

## THE RELATIONSHIP OF CHARACTERS

The very structure of *As I Lay Dying* manifests Faulkner's acceptance of the principle of human solidarity that holds the human race together. The fifteen characters who speak out during the course of the story exist primarily in their relationship to one another. Addie Bundren's death and funeral trip become the focal point, the historical event in which all these persons participate at differing levels of psychological involvement. As the Exodus is a type of everyman's wandering toward an elusive but ever-present God, so too the little world of the Bundrens is a paradigm of man's struggle to prevail.

Even in death Addie gives meaning to the actions of the other characters. Darl, Vardaman, Cash, Jewel, Dewey Dell, and Anse stand next to that inner circle which is Addie's alone. Around this family group stand the other characters, chorus-like in their function. Tull, Armstid, and Samson respond with actions to Anse's empty words; while Peabody interprets key actions and relates them to the outside world. Cora and Whitfield react to Addie's death with ethical words and phrases that border on the Pharisaical.[1] Only two char-

---

1. like the Pharisees, hypocritical and self-righteous biblical personages

acters are set outside the central action, entering the plot because of Dewey Dell's plight. . . .

## THE THEME OF SOLIDARITY

The basic supposition that makes such an intense interrela-
tion of these personalities possible is the solidarity of all
men. Theologically this solidarity arises from the doctrine
found in Genesis and in St. Paul's Epistle to the Romans (a
Christian commentary on this section of Genesis). Adam as
head of the race has sinned, and subsequent generations
have ratified Adam's sin in themselves by their personal
sins—thus sin, the power of darkness, reigns in the world.
All men are in Paul's words *tekna orgēs,* children of wrath.
Jewel explicitly symbolizes the child born in sin (like his
namesake Pearl in *The Scarlet Letter*); but he may also stand
as an unconscious symbol of that sinfulness in which all
men are born. It is not the sin of the person but the sin of the
race, of which the psalmist reminds us when he sings:
"Against thee, thee only have I sinned, and done that which
is evil in thy sight, so that thou art justified in thy sense, and
blameless in thy judgment. Behold I was brought forth in iniquity, and in sin did my mother conceive me" (Ps. 51:4-5).
The words remind us that within man continues to rage the
endless battle between the desire for salvation and an almost
primitive sense of guilt and sinfulness—something born into
us simply because we are men.

This sense of guilt is closely bound up with the sense of
solidarity and community because the impersonal guilt is
passed on through the sexual process. Hence Faulkner finds
it easy to link human solidarity with the mystery of woman
and sexuality. . . . The Old Testament parallels are striking:
Adam's sin is passed on through the sex act; the lives of the
great patriarchs turn around sexual experiences; the beget-
ting of children is a religious duty and yet a contaminated
process. The first book of the Bible, we might recall, is Genesis: the narration of God's creating and man's procreating.

As in the Old Testament accounts of the patriarchs, the life
cycle pervades *As I Lay Dying.* Even though Addie Bundren
lies on her death bed, her own flesh and blood, Dewey Dell,
carries within her womb the extension of Addie into space
and time. Dewey Dell's own involvement in the story frequently manifests itself in rich sensual imagery, imagery
that suggest the "womanliness" of nature. . . . Women sym-

bolize the quiet, immemorial, life-giving quality of the earth.

Furthermore, sex has traditionally been the basic concupiscence,[2] and historically Eve has borne more than her share of the blame for the Fall. Faulkner has committed himself to this theological tradition. This tension between man and woman flows in the background of *As I Lay Dying*, especially in Addie's treatment of Anse not as a subject but only as an object, a means whereby she tries to penetrate her loneliness. Twice she describes their courtship by saying, "so I took Anse."

For Faulkner, life depends on the fundamental experiences which can be reduced to man's struggle with the earth; the hatred, fear, and love, which prove a man in his relationship with a woman are paralleled by the hatred, fear, and love born of his struggle with the thorn and thistle-infested soil. The world of Yoknapatawpha differs little from the desert home of the biblical patriarchs, where life centers on tribal solidarity, sex, the search for food and water, and (not always clearly distinct from these for the patriarchs) salvation. Perhaps it is this fundamental parallel of man against the elements that makes the central action of *As I Lay Dying* appear so thoroughly biblical. Faulkner said he subjected this family to "the two greatest catastrophes man can suffer—flood and fire." Addie says that Jewel will save her from "the water and the fire" (not knowing how literally this would be fulfilled). This is also the psalmist's boast: "We went through fire and through water; but thou brought us forth to a spacious place" (Ps. 66:12).

## THE THEME OF REJECTION AND LONELINESS

In sharp contrast to the strong sense of tribal solidarity that we find in the Old Testament runs the parallel biblical theme of man's rejection and loneliness. Throughout scripture we find such laments as: "Turn unto me and have mercy on me, for I am lonely and afflicted" (Ps. 25:16). From the dark loneliness of her home-made coffin Addie could well cry out with the psalmist: "They surround me like a flood all day long: and they close in upon me together. Thou hast caused lover and friend to shun me; my companions are in darkness" (Ps. 88:17–18). Ironically, man finds himself alone amid the community. Like the chosen people of God who

2. lust

wandered for forty years through the desert, the Bundrens would make their journey trying to be "beholden to no man."

The very act which carries on the tribe in space and time has a dual aspect. Biologically speaking, it carries out its purpose with an impersonal relentlessness—pregnant women abound in the pages of Faulkner's stories. Humanly speaking, it should also be the "act of love," something personal that draws two people into a circle of mutual awareness. To the extent that it is not personal, another avenue of violating one's aloneness is sealed off. Addie Bundren represents the human desire to understand and be understood, to love and be loved in this act of love.

---

**ADDIE EXPRESSES THE SIN OF SOLIDARITY**

*In* As I Lay Dying, *Addie's vision of sin echoes the power of darkness that has reigned in the world since Adam's original sin.*

I believed that I had found it. . . . I would think of sin as I would think of the clothes we both wore in the world's face, of the circumspection necessary because he was he and I was I; the sin the more utter and terrible since he was the instrument ordained by God who created the sin, to sanctify that sin He had created. While I waited for [Anse] in the woods, waiting for him before he saw me, I would think of him as dressed in sin. I would think of him as thinking of me as dressed also in sin, he the more beautiful since the garment which he had exchanged for sin was sanctified. I would think of the sin as garments which we would remove in order to shape and coerce the terrible blood to the forlorn echo of the dead word high in the air. Then I would lay with Anse again—I did not lie to him: I just refused, just as I refused my breast to Cash and Darl after their time was up—hearing the dark land talking the voiceless speech.

---

From the opening pages of the book the reader is led deeper and deeper into the spirit of this lonely woman. Her husband says, "she was ever a private woman." The intense conflict between her independence and her desire for involvement permeate the story. Even in death Addie cannot break through her core of loneliness. Anse tells Cash—superficial though it may be coming from him—"We would be beholden to no man . . . me and her. We have never yet been, and she will rest quieter for knowing it and that it was her own blood sawed out the boards and drove the nails. She was ever one to clean up after herself.". . .

Even Addie's marriage to Anse, her ultimate attempt to surrender her aloneness, proved a failure. The surrender of the sex act, which nature intends in man as a balance for the inward pulling egocentricity, cannot satisfy Addie's thirst for awareness—for love, which was only a word to Anse. Her aloneness, she says, "had never been violated until Cash came. Not even by Anse in the night." She continues, "my aloneness had been violated and then made whole again by the violation: time, Anse, love, what you will, outside the circle."

This sense of alienation infects the whole Bundren clan. Jewel purchases the horse, an act symbolizing his alienation from the family of which he is only a partial member. Darl, chapter by chapter, fades into the twilight world of his brooding utterances about space, time, and existence.

Dewey Dell shares in this terrible conflict between aloneness and self-surrender: "It's because I am alone. If I could just feel it, it would be different, because I would not be alone. But if I were not alone, everybody would know it. And he [Peabody] could do so much for me, and then I would not be alone. Then I could be all right alone." This feeling mounts until she cries, "I feel my body, my bones and flesh beginning to part and open upon the alone, and the process of coming unalone is terrible."

Closely related, for example, to the theme of isolation and alienation is that of the worthlessness of mere words. This in turn opens out onto the constant rejection of hypocritical religious attitudes against which the Old Testament prophets preached for centuries. Thus, God through Jeremiah warned the people: "Amend your ways and your doings, and I will let you dwell in this place. Do not trust in these deceptive words: 'This is the temple of the Lord, the temple of the Lord, the temple of the Lord'" (Jer. 7:3-4). Of course, the prophet's reward for destroying the people's hope in mere words is alienation and rejection—loneliness in the midst of the tribe. Actions, not words will save Israel, just as actions, not words, will save Addie Bundren. Apart from such stray references as "a fallen sparrow, a log rising up like Christ walking on the waters," or Addie's statement that Jewel is her cross, there are few specifically Christian allusions in the story. These fragments are few in comparison to the many quotations and near quotations from the Old Testament. Ironically, most of this biblical language is spoken by the three most superficial and hypocritical characters in the book: Cora Tull, Whitfield, and Anse.

The book which comes most obviously to mind is the Book of Job. Even in structure the two stories are alike. Addie, like Job, rests in the center surrounded by her friends. Addie, like Job, finally rejects the words of those who do not really know what suffering is all about. The verbal parallels are striking. Several times, as we shall see, there are variations on Job's utterance: "Naked I came from my mother's womb, and naked shall I return; the Lord gave, and the Lord has taken away; blessed is the name of the Lord" (1:21). Anse frequently, and be it added hypocritically, assumes a Job-like pose. Twice, to Tull's "the Lord giveth," he laconically replies, "the Lord giveth." Three times he says, "if ever was such a misfortunate man." "It's a trial," he sighs, "but I don't begrudge her it." Knowing Jewel is outraged over his selling the horse, Anse laments, "I do the best I can. 'Fore God, if there were ere a man in the living world suffered the trials and floutings I have suffered."

Cora Tull is conventional religion incarnate. She has a tidbit of scripture to wrap around every one of her neighborly condemnations and rash judgments. Dewey Dell calls her "old turkey-buzzard Tull coming to watch her die." Jewel sees her joining with "them others [the women] sitting there like buzzards"—like Job's friends gathering around him. Anse, too, is infected with this meaningless spirit, a belief without any seeming personal commitment or involvement. When Addie dies there rises from his soul the anguished cry: "God's will be done. . . . Now I can get them teeth."

However, no character in the story presents a more pathetic picture of religiosity and the emptiness of words than does Whitfield. We first see him after he has safely crossed the river on his way to pray over the dying Addie. His prayer, it might be noted in passing, is a perfect imitation of the repetitive structure of the psalms: "It was His hand that bore me safely above the flood, that fended from me the dangers of the waters.". . .

Through the persons of Vernon Tull and Addie Bundren, Faulkner rejects this religious posing. Tull at one point challenges Cora's "theologizing" and shows her to be ironically contradicting herself. . . . Addie, more deeply involved in the central movement of the story, has an even more telling criticism of such religiosity: "One day I was talking to Cora. She prayed for me because she believed I was blind to sin, wanting me to kneel and pray too, because people to whom sin is just a matter of words, to them salvation is just words too." Like Job, Addie is surrounded by her friends—people who talk much of sin and suffering and salvation; yet their hearts are unexperienced, untried. Her only chapter in the novel is preceded by one of Cora's and immediately followed by Whitfield's only chapter. Job, hemmed in and thoroughly tired of his advisers, dourly remarks: "Worthless physicians are you all. . . . Your maxims are proverbs of ashes" (13:4, 12). In the same spirit Addie says:

> And so when Cora Tull would tell me I was not a true mother, I would think how words go straight up in a thin line, quick and harmless, and how terribly doing goes along the earth, clinging to it, so that after a while the two lines are too far apart for the same person to straddle from one to the other; and that sin and love and fear are just sounds that people who never sinned nor loved have for what they never had and cannot have until they forget the words. Like Cora, who could never even cook.

This comes close to being the principal theme of *As I Lay Dying.*

Addie is concerned about her salvation—she is concerned about love and belonging—and it seems to be the salvation through endurance and suffering that runs throughout Faulkner's other stories. Addie sees her redemption bound up in some confused way with her relationship with Whitfield. When Cora, unaware of Jewel's true father, tells Addie "Jewel is your punishment. But where is your salvation?" Addie replies, "he is my cross and he will be my salvation. He will save me from the water and from the fire. Even though I have laid down my life, he will save me."

The vision is not clear, at least theologically speaking; but Addie herself says, in trying to explain her terrible sense of aloneness, "I learned that words are no good; that words don't ever fit even what they are trying to say at." Yet how closely, even verbally, her retort to Cora matches Job's cry of hope in the face of the seemingly unjust trials inflicted upon him: "For I know that my Redeemer lives, and at last he will stand upon the earth; And after my skin has been thus destroyed, then from my flesh I shall see God" (19:25–26). The full Christian vision does not enter the picture. Just as Faulkner does not resolve the paradox of aloneness in the face of solidarity, so he does not offer a solution to the problem of salvation. The human heart aches in *As I Lay Dying* and later novels, but its yearning is not calmed by the clear promise of intimate union with a personal redeemer. The hope is vague and distant—as it is in the Old Testament. His message is the Old Testament message of Job: "Naked I came from my mother's womb and naked shall I return."

Even when tempered by irony and hope and folk-humor the feeling is still present that man must face the mystery of life alone—naked before God and his fellow men. . . . Riding to Jefferson, Dewey Dell says, "I sit naked on the seat above the unhurrying mules, above the travail." Finally, Peabody looks at the dying Addie and reflects—in what is almost a modern paraphrase of Job's utterance—"That's what they mean by the love that passeth understanding: that pride, that furious desire to hide that abject nakedness which we bring here with us, carry with us into the operating rooms, carry stubbornly and furiously into the earth again."

## THE DESTINY TO SUFFER AND STRUGGLE, BUT TO PREVAIL

The vision is troubled and strained, because it is man's lot to be caught up in an enigmatic existence: both spirit and matter, man is destined to suffer in the midst of plenty, to be lonely in the multitude of his relationships, to achieve life through death. For Faulkner it is a world in which life is predominantly a struggle, but a struggle in which victory is at least a possibility and not a mere velleity.[3]

One feels at journey's end that the battered contingent sitting on the wagon eating bananas may yet survive: Cash will have a graphophone to listen to; Dewey Dell in her sullen way will have the child; shrewd old Anse has his new teeth and a new Mrs. Bundren; even Darl, Cash reflects, will be better off: "It is better so for him. This world is not his world; this life his life."

Twenty years after writing *As I Lay Dying* Faulkner could still sound the note of hope that flows through his books: "I believe that man will not merely endure: he will prevail. He is immortal, not because he alone among creatures has an inexhaustible voice, but because he has a soul, a spirit capable of compassion and sacrifice and endurance."[4]

3. wish or inclination    4. from his speech accepting the Nobel Prize

# The Three Narratives of *Light in August*

Richard Chase

Richard Chase explains the three characters whose narratives loosely interconnect in *Light in August.* Chase describes self-assured Lena Grove as a contrast to Joe Christmas, whose divided self lacks identity, and Reverend Hightower, whose obsessive identification with his Confederate grandfather has ruined his life. Though the characters barely interact, Chase shows that Hightower brings them together and unifies the novel. Richard Chase earned his doctorate from Columbia University, where he taught English for many years. He is the author of books on American writers Herman Melville, Emily Dickinson, and Walt Whitman.

In *Light in August* things are perceived in space rather than temporally as they are in *The Sound and the Fury.* Except for the Reverend Hightower, one of Faulkner's characters who are ruined by time, no one is particularly aware of time; and the surviving, enduring character, Lena Grove, lives in a timeless realm which seems to be at once eternity and the present moment. The Mississippi landscape spreads out before us and the faculty of vision becomes very important as we are shown the town of Jefferson, the houses of Hightower and Miss Burden, or the smoke on the horizon as Miss Burden's house burns. . . .

Lena Grove, a poor and ignorant farm girl from Alabama, painfully wends her way into northern Mississippi in pursuit of Lucas Burch, with whose child she is pregnant. Hearing that her ne'er-do-well lover has got a job at a sawmill near Jefferson, she goes there and finds Byron Bunch and Joe Christmas. But Burch has left; as the story goes on, Lena has her child and at the end is still on the road, an example apparently of perpetual motion. Now she is accompanied not by Burch but by Bunch; which one accompanies her she seems to regard as a matter of indifference.

Meanwhile in a long and exhaustive flash-back we are told the history of Joe Christmas, an orphan and (as everyone including himself assumes) part Negro. We are told how Christmas murders Miss Burden, a descendant of New England abolitionists, and how he is caught, escapes, and is finally murdered himself in the Reverend Hightower's kitchen by Percy Grimm. We are also told a good deal about the life of Hightower, particularly how he ruined his career and lost his wife because of his fantasy of identification with his Confederate grandfather, an officer in the army who had been killed in Jefferson during the Civil War. As the story unfolds, Hightower is now an old man isolated from the world, but before he dies he gets more or less involved with Lena and Joe Christmas and serves rather loosely as the unifying figure and center of intelligence of the last sections of the novel. There are thus three separate strands of narrative in *Light in August,* each having its central character. The book makes a kind of triptych.

## LENA GROVE

Lena Grove is one of those intensely female females we meet in Faulkner's books, like Eula Varner in *The Hamlet.* A somewhat bovine earth mother, she has all those womanly qualities which, as Faulkner likes to point out, baffle, fascinate, outrage, and finally defeat men. According to Faulkner's gynecological demonology (it constitutes a sort of Mississippi Manichaeism[1]) men are more interesting and valuable than women but the dark or Satanic principle of the universe decrees that they are the weaker sex and are doomed to be frustrated and ephemeral. . . .

The bovine woman brings to Faulkner's mind echoes of ancient myth and ritual (hence the name, Lena Grove—cf. Hilma Tree in *The Octopus*) and he treats her alternately with gravity and with a measure of humorously grandiose fantasy and mockery. Lena's placidity is not only that of the cow but unmistakably that of the gods in their eternity. Hence Faulkner has given her a ritual office by associating her with the religious procession depicted in Keats's "Ode on

1. a dualistic philosophy dividing the world between good and evil principles

a Grecian Urn," a favorite poem of Faulkner of which there are several echoes in *Light in August.* In Lena's unvarying inner harmony (and here Faulkner is serious rather than mocking) all opposites and disparates are reconciled or perhaps rendered meaningless. In the words of Keats's poem, beauty is truth and truth beauty. By implying that Lena Grove somehow symbolizes this ideal unity Faulkner suggests no metaphysical reconciliation. He merely praises again the quiet enduring stoicism and wisdom of the heart which he finds among the poor whites, Negroes, and other socially marginal types.

## JOE CHRISTMAS

The first thing to be said about Joe Christmas is that he is not a villain, as is sometimes thought. Nor, except in a distantly symbolic way, is he a tragic hero or a "Christ-figure." He has many of the qualities Faulkner admires. He suffers, he is a divided man, he is marginal and bereaved; he is "outraged." He asks merely to live, to share the human experience, and to be an individual. Like the slave in "Red Leaves," he "runs well"—he has in other words some power of giving his doomed life meaning by insisting as long as he can on his right to be human. All this outbalances his being a criminal. It even outbalances his being a murderer.

It is the custom of some traditionalist critics to say, in the words of one of them, that "sentimentalists and sociologists are bound to regard Christmas solely as a victim," whereas actually he is a tragic figure akin to Oedipus. But the main difference between Joe Christmas and Oedipus (or any other tragic hero in the full classic sense) is that Christmas really *is* a victim; he never has a chance, and a chance, or at least the illusion of a chance, a tragic hero must have. . . .

What happens later to Joe Christmas is made inevitable by the circumstances of his boyhood in the orphanage. In fact one may be very specific about the origin of the train of causes. Christmas's life is given its definitive bias by his encounter with the dietitian, described near the beginning of Chapter 6. Hiding in a closet and eating toothpaste, he has seen the dietitian making illicit love. When she discovers this, Christmas expects, and *desires*, to be whipped. Instead she offers him a silver dollar:

> He was waiting to get whipped and then be released. Her voice went on, urgent, tense, fast: "A whole dollar. See? How

> much you could buy. Some to eat every day for a week. And
> next month maybe I'll give you another one."

> He did not move or speak. He might have been carven, as a
> large toy: small, still, round headed and round eyed, in over-
> alls. He was still with astonishment, shock, outrage.

What the boy wants is recognition, acceptance as a human
being, if only through physical punishment. A whipping
would establish the passionate, human contact. Instead he is
given a silver dollar, and he sees his doom in its adamant,
abstract, circular form. He has now been given an irre-
sistible compulsion to destroy every human relationship that
he gets involved in. And this compulsion includes the suicidal desire to destroy himself.

Joe Christmas thus joins the long procession of isolated,
doomed heroes that begin to appear in the American novel
with Brockden Brown, Hawthorne, and Melville. . . . Apparently nothing appears to our American novelists to be more
terrible than to have become isolated or to have fallen victim
to a cold, abstract hatred of life—nor, we must admit, does
any doom call forth a more spontaneous admiration or require a more arduous repudiation. . . .

## REVEREND HIGHTOWER

The Reverend Hightower is one of Faulkner's best characters. He appeals to us in many ways—first and most impor-
tantly in the sad everyday conditions of his life: the decaying
house with the weather-beaten sign in front saying "Art
Lessons Christmas Cards Photographs Developed"; the
swivel chair in which he sits before the desk with the green
shaded reading lamp as he gazes fixedly out the window; his
moving colloquies with Byron Bunch, who, though his companion, is so different from him in heritage and intellect—as
different as Sancho Panza is from Don Quixote (a parallel
which is very much in Faulkner's mind). Only because
Hightower is established in novelistic detail do we become
interested in the fantastic obsession that has ruined his life.
Like Quentin Compson and Horace Benbow (see *Sartoris*
and *Sanctuary*), Hightower is one of Faulkner's intellectuals—he is fastidious, genteel, frightened by life. Haunted by
the glory and crime of the past, he is incapable of living in
the present. Like Quentin Compson he tries willfully to im-
pose a kind of order on the irrational flow of time and nature. His view of things, however, is not metaphysical or the-

ological like Quentin's; it is purely mythic and aesthetic, the product of a mind immersed in Keats and Tennyson. A careful reading of the pages at the end of Chapter 20 will show that Hightower does not return to his earlier Christian belief in his moment of ultimate insight before he dies. The turn of his mind is to grasp truth aesthetically; truth is for him an ecstatic perception of a supreme moment in the natural, historical order, a moment in which, to employ the Keatsian vocabulary Faulkner encourages us to use, beauty is grasped as truth and truth as beauty. Before he dies he sees the truth about himself—"I have not been clay"—which is merely a way of admitting finally that neither truth nor beauty can be perceived by the mind that remains inverted and solipsistic[2] and denies man's common fate in nature and time. This is the truth that finally comes to Hightower; and it is what allows him to see for the first time, and pathetically for the last, the full beauty of the myth he has lived by. For a moment he can now be free, for the first time and the last. The progression of his views has thus taken him beyond his Christianity and his pure aestheticism to a full, profound, perhaps tragic naturalism.

2. the belief that the self is the only reality

# The Framelike Structure of *Light in August*

Alan Warren Friedman

Alan Warren Friedman argues that the actions and character of Lena Grove, whose story begins and ends *Light in August*, frame the stories of Joe Christmas, Joanna Burden, and Gail Hightower. Friedman maintains that while Lena's continuous journey symbolizes the progression of the seasons, the other characters move in circles repeating their past failures. Alan Warren Friedman has taught English at the University of Texas in Austin. He is the editor of *Forms of Modern British Fiction* and has contributed to *Seven Contemporary Authors* and to numerous scholarly journals.

*Light in August* is unique among Faulkner's novels not in its obsessive, reiterated failures but in the framing context in which its gothic horrors occur: kindliness, serenity, motion that is linear and progressive, natural fecundity. The novel begins and ends with Lena Grove—first pregnant then, lighter in August, a mother—as she journeys, aided only by the instinctive generosity of strangers, from Alabama to Mississippi (where the novel's action occurs) and then to Tennessee. Tracking Lucas Burch, her baby's father, she seems almost indifferent to his fleeing from her when they finally meet in the novel as he had after impregnating her. Her serenity, in fact, is threatened only when, right after the birth, it seems that she might actually reclaim Lucas and lose Byron Bunch, the novel's quixotic hero who, on sight, falls hopelessly in love with her. By the end, Lucas has come to seem far more traveling's excuse than its goal, the putative quest for respectability allowing Lena—as the amused furniture dealer who narrates the last chapter in bed to his wife expresses it—"to travel a little further and see as much as she could, since I reckon she knew that when she settled down this time, it would likely be for the rest of her life."

Settling down, domesticity, is exactly what fails all of the other major characters in the novel, and vice versa; burdened with inherited visions of disaster and doom, they are incapable of defining viable roles for themselves as spouses, parents, or children. They remain outsiders, strangers, wherever they live, and consequently destroy those closest to them and themselves. Lacking the immediacy of parental influence, Joe Christmas, Joanna Burden, and the Reverend Gail Hightower are all literally or figuratively haunted by monomaniacal grandfathers who seem bent on denying them the unique origins and individuality common to the rest of humankind.

## THE MISTREATMENT OF JOE CHRISTMAS

Faulkner has said that he began the novel with the placid image of Lena en route to give birth but that Christmas, most obsessed of all his characters with his origins and most ignorant of them, defines "the tragic, central idea of the story—that he didn't know what he was, and there was no way possible in life for him to find out.". . .

His grandfather Hines, we learn late in the novel, had killed his daughter's lover because he was convinced he had black blood; he then refused his daughter a doctor, and so caused her to die in childbirth. Left on the doorstep of an orphanage on Christmas eve, the baby received the name that marks him as an alien, a pariah, all his life:

> "Is he a foreigner?"
> "Did you ever hear of a white man named Christmas?" the foreman said.
> "I never heard of nobody a-tall named it," the other said.

Joe's years in the orphanage are literally watched over "with a profound and unflagging attention" by the "mad eyes" of Hines whose presence, as janitor, thus sets Joe apart from the other children, who ridicule him with the taunt of "nigger." Adopted at the age of five by the Calvinist Simon McEachern, Joe moves from one religious fanaticism to another. Enduring a harsh upbringing (he is beaten when he fails, or refuses, to learn the catechism), he acquires neither self-understanding nor knowledge of how to survive in a world of ambivalent demands and offers, but only the self-stigmatizing label "nigger" that he claims for himself at the most inconvenient times. When actually asked directly, however, he acknowledges ignorance, and then wryly adds, "If I'm not, damned if I wasted haven't a lot of time."

Not surprisingly, Joe's greatest failures are with females, whom he finds totally unpredictable and, therefore, untrustworthy. . . . Joanna Burden whose fierce carnality had corrupted *him* for two years and whose subsequent religiosity, arousing old desperation, spurs him to murder her and leads to his own death. . . . No character in the book plunges more desperately than Joe into both thought and action; but, remaining peripheral and fragmented, he never manages to make them cohere.

## THE MISTREATMENT OF JOANNA BURDEN

Though Joanna Burden, too, ultimately seeks to have her will of him, her story strongly parallels Joe's and is inextricably linked to it. She has lived all her life in the house in which "she was born, yet she is still a stranger, a foreigner whose people moved in from the North during Reconstruction." Like Joe's, her grandfather, aptly named Calvin Burden, had killed in self-righteous defense of his beliefs and bullied his family about hell and damnation, beating "the loving God" into his children. Murdered along with Joanna's brother by Colonel Sartoris for defending Negro voting rights after the Civil War, he leaves Joanna burdened by his passion and vision. She devotes herself not only to improving Negro education throughout the South, but also to assisting neighboring blacks who bring her their personal problems. She is, in fact, shunned locally as a "nigger lover"—though as soon as her death is discovered, the town righteously determines to lynch *her* "nigger lover." Like Joe, Joanna continually initiates the actions that victimize her: her rape by Joe, their violent and corrupting sensuality, her death. . . .

Although we learn this later, Joe's murder of Joanna and his setting fire to her house occur almost exactly as the novel begins, for Lena's first sight of Jefferson the next morning is of a sky filled with smoke. The murder, is in fact, one of those key Faulknerian moments that is always past or imminent but never present, always envisioned or revised rather than actually represented. Thus, the image of that smoke—"impregnable as a monument"—pervades the novel's present even before we know its significance, and the murder is recounted by several characters, none of whom witnessed it. . . .

Joe, then, is both free and trapped. He is released for flight with the death of Joanna's corrupting constraints, relieved of responsibility for a murder that she and fate willed and contrived, beyond time's orderly progression (as indicated by sudden shifts in verb tenses) and such regular needs as food and sleep. Yet his journey, unlike Lena's, is circular, regressive. Hers is predicated on self-knowledge and serendipity, openness to new experience; his is a desperate hurtling toward certitude and identity that, once found, will both define and doom him. . . .

Only in journey's end does this lost soul—who could live neither within nor "outside the human race"—achieve a Lena-like harmony and meaning, for his memory, we are told, "will be there, musing, quiet, steadfast, not fading and not particularly threatful, but of itself alone serene, of itself alone triumphant."

## HIGHTOWER'S FAILURES AND ULTIMATE AWARENESS

Gail Hightower's is yet another version of the novel's central story, and since it is told in the novel's third and penultimate chapters, it serves as a kind of double counterpoint: a frame within a frame. Like Joe and Joanna, Hightower inherits and inhabits a grandfather's vision rather than imagines one of his own—"as though the seed which his grandfather had transmitted to him had been on the horse too that night and had been killed too and time had stopped there and then for the seed and nothing had happened in time since, not even him." He came to Jefferson as "toward the consummation of his life," it being where his swashbuckling grandfather had died, only to fail disastrously himself: "It was as if he couldn't get religion and that galloping cavalry and his dead grandfather shot from the galloping horse untangled from each other, even in the pulpit." Having first driven his wife to madness, illicit sex, and suicide, and then lost both his church and *the* Church, Hightower refuses to leave Jefferson even after he is threatened and beaten. Byron knows what holds him: "A man will talk about how he'd like to escape from living folks. But it's the dead folks that do him the damage. It's the dead ones that lay quiet in one place and dont try to hold him, that he can't escape from." Like Joe, Hightower had vainly sought a separate peace, the kind implicit in the surname half of his divided self: "it seemed to him that he could see his future, his life, intact and on all sides complete and inviolable, like a classic and serene vase, where the spirit could be born anew sheltered from the harsh *gale* of living" (my italics). But this ethereal self-image clashes impossibly with Hightower's failure to find peace and meaning in being the son of his father, a man of contradictions whose actions often negated his coldly uncompromising convictions. He was "a minister without a church and a soldier without an enemy," whose abhorrence of slavery compelled him neither to "eat food grown and cooked by, nor sleep in a bed prepared by, a negro slave" but which somehow allowed him to participate––albeit as a noncombatant—in the long and bloody struggle to perpetuate slavery. He lived a life that, for Hightower, was devoid of purpose and, therefore, no more real for him than Joanna's father was for her. Instead, like Faulkner's South itself, Hightower expresses a forlorn, prelapsarian[1] identity, "full of galloping cavalry and defeat and glory," one associated with his grandfather's "swagger, his bluff and simple adherence to a simple code." "'So it's no wonder,' he thinks, 'that I skipped a generation. It's no wonder that I had no father and that I had already died one night twenty years before I saw light. And that my only salvation must be to return to the place to die where my life had already ceased before it began.'"

But Hightower's story becomes a repetition with a difference, for unlike Joe and Joanna he undergoes a kind of gestation during the course of the novel. Recipient of Byron's confidences and startling news about Lena and Christmas, Hightower at first remains passive and then rejects reinvolving himself in human affairs: "I am not in life anymore." Furthermore, he urges Byron to flee Lena and mocks him as "the guardian of public weal and morality." But in the end, and despite his name and instincts, Gail Hightower is neither obsessed nor aloof; he responds not only to Byron's goodness but to Byron's evocation of his own: he silently blesses Byron for ignoring his advice, successfully delivers Lena's baby, and later tries to save Joe after earlier having refused to do so. After the birth Hightower feels triumphant and purposeful for the first time in twenty-five years ("Life comes to the old man yet"), foresees many more babies for Lena—by Byron, and mourns Joanna: "Poor, barren woman.

1. naive, unaware

To have not lived only a week longer, until luck returned to this place." And though he weeps like a newborn at his forced reentry into life, he finally does what Joe never could: confronts the truth about his grandfather (a murderer and a chicken thief) and about what he had done to his wife: "I became her seducer and her murderer, author and instrument of her shame and death." He had offered his congregation, he now realizes, not pity and love but "a swaggering and unchastened bravo killed with a shotgun in a peaceful henhouse, in a temporary hiatus of his own avocation of killing." The book's last view of Hightower is ambiguous, for, thinking he is dying, he hears again "the wild bugles and the clashing sabres and the dying thunder of hooves"—though it may be that Hightower does survive (as Faulkner insists in an interview) while the sound in his head finally dies, and that he is at last free to envision some viable identity of his own.

## LENA'S STORY AS A FRAME

The novel ends more or less where it began—with Lena Grove on the road, passively bemused by experience, reiterating her sense of wonder and openness: "My, my. A body does get around"—though now toting her infant and accompanied by Byron who *"had done desperated himself up"* enough to cast his lot with her. The novel began with a tableau, a vision of terrific immobility: "Sitting beside the road, watching the wagon mount the hill toward her, Lena thinks, 'I have come from Alabama: a fur piece. All the way from Alabama a-walking. A fur piece.' Thinking..."—the four present participles in the first four lines serving to link active and passive modes, action and contemplation, momentum and stasis—inertia in both its senses. The language associated with Lena throughout has this same double quality: "Her voice is quiet, dogged. Yet it is serene"; "Her face is calm as stone, but not hard," tranquil and hearty decorum"; "serene pride"; "interested, tranquil"—the language not of tidal waves or hurricanes, but of "the untroubled unhaste of a change of season": incremental, unnoticed, inevitable. Her journey is "like something moving forever and without progress across an urn," almost a reversal of motion: "backrolling now behind her a long monotonous succession of peaceful and undeviating changes from day to dark and dark to day again." She and the wagon that is about to contain her "draw slowly together as the wagon crawls terrifically toward her in its slow palpable aura of somnolence and red dust." And with her in it, "The wagon goes on, slow, timeless."

The vision is one compounded of intense summer heat, vast quantities of dust, and "a lambence, a luminous quality to the light, as though it came not from just today but from back in the old classic times. It might have fauns and satyrs and the gods. . . . Maybe the connection was with Lena Grove, who had something of that pagan quality of being able to assume everything." Lena represents not the obsessive repetition of past failures—as do Christmas, Burden, and Hightower—but the repetition of seasons, waves, fecundity, the reiterated ancient rhythms that endure man's violence and disasters. Lena's story and vision do not, unfortunately, negate these others, but they provide them a structural and thematic context, a mode of containment. Faulkner takes a great risk here, for we might be tempted to assume that Lena's unreflective and sheeplike progress is meant as a moral exemplum; but he is not so simple as to advocate that we eschew evil and self-destruction by becoming as are the beasts of the fields. Lena is, after all, more comic caricature than believable character, an assurance that life has its triumphs despite, if not because, of all man's efforts. It may be a weakness of *Light in August*—as the most common criticism of the book maintains—that its contradictory stories live together most uncomfortably, but this is no truer within its confines than outside of them.

# CHAPTER 4

# Major Works After 1932

READINGS ON

WILLIAM FAULKNER

# Absalom, Absalom! as a Legend of the Deep South

Malcolm Cowley

Malcolm Cowley argues that *Absalom, Absalom!* is a legend about southerners in the post–Civil War era who try to restore their prewar way of life, but who find themselves displaced by a new class of whites who exploit and corrupt the South. Cowley introduces the narrator of the story, Quentin Compson, who tells the story of Thomas Sutpen to his Ohio roommate in a Harvard University dorm room. The incredulousness of the roomate emphasizes the essence of the South that Faulkner portrays. Educated at Harvard University, Malcolm Cowley became an expatriate in France during the 1920s. He is the author of two volumes of poems, the translator of French books into English, and the author of many works on major American writers.

All his books in the Yoknapatawpha saga are part of the same living pattern. . . . Although the pattern is presented in terms of a single Mississippi county, it can be extended to the Deep South as a whole; and Faulkner always seems conscious of its wider application. . . .

The story he tells—I am trying to summarize the plot of *Absalom, Absalom!*—is that of a mountain boy named Thomas Sutpen whose family drifted into the Virginia lowlands, where his father found odd jobs on a plantation. One day the father sent him with a message to the big house, but he was turned away at the door by a black man in livery. Puzzled and humiliated, the mountain boy was seized upon by the lifelong ambition to which he would afterward refer as "the design." He too would own a plantation with slaves and a liveried butler; he would build a mansion as big as any of those in the

From the Introduction by Malcolm Cowley to *The Portable Faulkner*, edited by Malcolm Cowley. Copyright 1946, ©1966, 1967 by The Viking Press, Inc., renewed. Used by permission of Viking Penguin, a division of Penguin Books USA Inc.

Tidewater; and he would have a son to inherit his wealth.

A dozen years later, Sutpen appeared in the frontier town of Jefferson, where he managed to obtain a hundred square miles of land from the Chickasaws. With the help of twenty wild Negroes from the jungle and a French architect, he set about building the largest house in northern Mississippi, using timbers from the forest and bricks that his Negroes molded and baked on the spot; it was as if his mansion, Sutpen's Hundred, had been literally torn from the soil. Only one man in Jefferson—he was Quentin's grandfather, General Compson—ever learned how and where Sutpen had acquired his slaves. He had shipped to Haiti from Virginia, worked as overseer on a sugar plantation and married the rich planter's daughter, who had borne him a son. Then, finding that his wife had Negro blood, he had simply put her away, with her child and her fortune, while keeping the twenty slaves as a sort of indemnity.

In Jefferson, Sutpen married again. This time his wife belonged to a pious family of the neighborhood, and she bore him two children, Henry and Judith. He became the biggest cotton planter in Yoknapatawpha County, and it seemed that his "design" had already been fulfilled. At this moment, however, Henry came home from the University of Mississippi with an older and worldlier new friend, Charles Bon, who was in reality Sutpen's son by his first marriage. Charles became engaged to Judith. Sutpen learned his identity and, without making a sign of recognition, ordered him from the house. Henry, who refused to believe that Charles was his half-brother, renounced his birthright and followed him to New Orleans. In 1861, all the male Sutpens went off to war, and all of them survived four years of fighting. Then, in the spring of 1865, Charles suddenly decided to marry Judith, even though he was certain by now that she was his half-sister. Henry rode beside him all the way back to Sutpen's Hundred, but tried to stop him at the gate, killed him when he insisted on going ahead with his plan, told Judith what he had done, and disappeared.

But Quentin's story of the Deep South does not end with the war. Colonel Sutpen came home, he says, to find his wife dead, his son a fugitive, his slaves dispersed (they had run away even before they were freed by the Union army), and most of his land about to be seized for debt. Still determined to carry out "the design," he did not even pause for breath before undertaking to restore his house and plantation to what they had been. The effort failed and Sutpen was reduced to keeping a crossroads store. Now in his sixties, he tried again to beget a son; but his wife's younger sister, Miss Rosa Coldfield, was outraged by his proposal ("Let's try it," he had said, "and if it's a boy we'll get married"); and later poor Milly Jones, with whom he had an affair, gave birth to a baby girl. At that Sutpen abandoned hope and provoked Milly's grandfather into killing him. Judith survived her father for a time, as did the half-caste son of Charles Bon by a New Orleans octoroon. After the death of these two by yellow fever, the great house was haunted rather than inhab-

---

## A Genealogy of Characters in *Absalom, Absalom!*

*The following list identifies major characters in* Absalom, Absalom! *along with their birth and death dates and places.*

THOMAS SUTPEN. Born in West Virginia mountains, 1807. One of several children of poor whites, Scotch-English stock. Established plantation of Sutpen's Hundred in Yoknapatawpha County, Mississippi, 1833. Married (1) Eulalia Bon, Haiti, 1827. (2) Ellen Coldfield, Jefferson, Mississippi, 1838. Major, later Colonel, —th Mississippi Infantry, C.S.A. Died, Sutpen's Hundred, 1869.

EULALIA BON. Born in Haiti. Only child of Haitian sugar planter of French descent. Married Thomas Sutpen, 1827, divorced from him, 1831. Died in New Orleans, date unknown.

CHARLES BON. Son of Thomas and Eulalia Bon Sutpen. Only child. Attended University of Mississippi, where he met Henry Sutpen and became engaged to Judith. Private, later lieutenant,—th Company, (University Greys) —th Mississippi Infantry, C.S.A. Died, Sutpen's Hundred, 1865.

GOODHUE COLDFIELD. Born in Tennessee. Moved to Jefferson, Miss., 1828, established small mercantile business. Died, Jefferson, 1864.

ELLEN COLDFIELD. Daughter of Goodhue Coldfield. Born in Tennessee, 1818. Married Thomas Sutpen, Jefferson, Miss., 1838. Died, Sutpen's Hundred, 1862.

ROSA COLDFIELD. Daughter of Goodhue Coldfield. Born, Jefferson, 1845. Died, Jefferson, 1910.

HENRY SUTPEN. Born, Sutpen's Hundred, 1839, son of Thomas and Ellen Coldfield Sutpen. Attended University of Mississippi. Private,—th Company, (University Greys)—th Mississippi Infantry, C.S.A. Died, Sutpen's Hundred, 1910.

ited by an ancient mulatto woman, Sutpen's daughter by one of his slaves. The fugitive Henry Sutpen came home to die; the townspeople heard of his illness and sent an ambulance after him; but old Clytie thought they were arresting him for murder and set fire to Sutpen's Hundred. The only survival of the conflagration was Jim Bond, a half-witted creature who was Charles Bon's grandson.

"Now I want you to tell me just one thing more," Shreve McCannon says after hearing the story. "Why do you hate the South?"—"I don't hate it," Quentin says quickly, at once. "I don't hate it," he repeats, speaking for the author as well as himself. *I don't hate it*, he thinks, panting in the cold air,

JUDITH SUTPEN. Daughter of Thomas and Ellen Coldfield Sutpen. Born, Sutpen's Hundred, 1841. Became engaged to Charles Bon, 1860. Died, Sutpen's Hundred, 1884.

CLYTEMNESTRA SUTPEN. Daughter of Thomas Sutpen and a negro slave. Born, Sutpen's Hundred, 1834. Died, Sutpen's Hundred, 1910.

WASH JONES. Date and location of birth unknown. Squatter, residing in an abandoned fishing camp belonging to Thomas Sutpen, hanger-on of Sutpen, handy man about Sutpen's place while Sutpen was away between '61–'65. Died, Sutpen's Hundred, 1869.

MELICENT JONES. Daughter of Wash Jones. Date of birth unknown. Rumored to have died in a Memphis brothel.

MILLY JONES. Daughter of Melicent Jones. Born 1853. Died, Sutpen's Hundred, 1869.

UNNAMED INFANT. Daughter of Thomas Sutpen and Milly Jones. Born, died, Sutpen's Hundred, same day, 1869.

CHARLES ETIENNE DE SAINT VELERY BON. Only child of Charles Bon and an octoroon mistress whose name is not recorded. Born, New Orleans, 1859. Married a full-blood negress, name unknown, 1879. Died, Sutpen's Hundred, 1884.

JIM BOND (BON). Son of Charles Etienne de Saint Velery Bon. Born, Sutpen's Hundred, 1882. Disappeared from Sutpen's Hundred, 1910. Whereabouts unknown.

QUENTIN COMPSON. Grandson of Thomas Sutpen's first Yoknapatawpha County friend. Born, Jefferson, 1891. Attended Harvard, 1909–1910. Died, Cambridge, Mass., 1910.

SHREVLIN MCCANNON. Born, Edmonton, Alberta, Canada, 1890. Attended Harvard, 1909–1914. Captain, Royal Army Medical Corps, Canadian Expeditionary Forces, France, 1914–1918. Now a practising surgeon, Edmonton, Alta.

the iron New England dark; *I don't. I don't hate it! I don't hate it!*[1]

The reader cannot help wondering why this somber and, at moments, plainly incredible story had so seized upon Quentin's mind that he trembled with excitement when telling it and felt that it revealed the essence of the Deep South. It seems to belong in the realm of Gothic romances, with Sutpen's Hundred taking the place of the haunted castle on the Rhine, with Colonel Sutpen as Faust and Charles Bon as Manfred. Then slowly it dawns on you that most of the characters and incidents have a double meaning; that besides their place in the story, they also serve as symbols or metaphors with a general application. Sutpen's great design, the land he stole from the Indians, the French architect who built his house with the help of wild Negroes from the jungle, the woman of mixed blood whom he married and disowned, the unacknowledged son who ruined him, the poor white whom he wronged and who killed him in anger, the final destruction of the mansion like the downfall of a social order: all these might belong to a tragic fable of Southern history. With a little cleverness, the whole novel might be explained as a connected and logical allegory, but this, I think, would be going far beyond the author's intention. First of all he was writing a story, and one that affected him deeply, but he was also brooding over a social situation. More or less unconsciously, the incidents in the story came to represent the forces and elements in the social situation, since the mind naturally works in terms of symbols and parallels. In Faulkner's case, this form of parallelism is not confined to *Absalom, Absalom!* It can be found in the whole fictional framework that he has been elaborating in novel after novel, until his work has become a myth or legend of the South.

I call it a legend because it is obviously no more intended as a historical account of the country south of the Ohio than *The Scarlet Letter* was intended as a history of Massachusetts or *Paradise Lost* as a factual description of the Fall. Briefly stated, the legend might run something like this: The Deep South was settled partly by aristocrats like the Sartoris clan and partly by new men like Colonel Sutpen. Both types of planters were determined to establish a lasting social order on the land they had seized from the Indians (that is,

1. last lines in *Absalom, Absalom!*

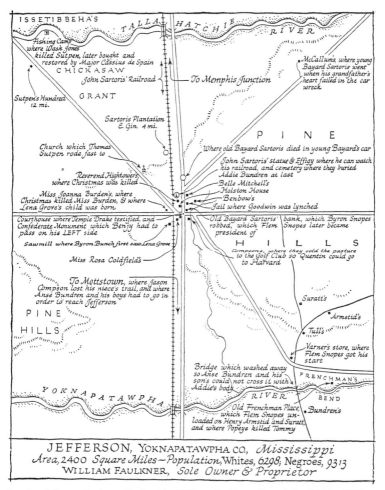

JEFFERSON, YOKNAPATAWPHA CO., *Mississippi*
*Area,* 2400 *Square Miles — Population,* Whites, 6298; Negroes, 9313
WILLIAM FAULKNER, *Sole Owner & Proprietor*

to leave sons behind them). They had the virtue of living single-mindedly by a fixed code; but there was also an inherent guilt in their "design," their way of life; it was slavery that put a curse on the land and brought about the Civil War. After the War was lost, partly as a result of their own mad heroism (for who else but men as brave as Jackson and Stuart could have frightened the Yankees into standing together and fighting back?) they tried to restore "the design" by other methods. But they no longer had the strength to achieve more than a partial success, even after they had freed their land from the carpetbaggers who followed the Northern armies. As time passed, moreover, the men of the old order found that they had Southern enemies too: they had to fight against a new exploiting class descended from the landless whites of slavery days. In this struggle between the clan of Sartoris and the unscrupulous tribe of Snopes, the Sartorises were defeated in advance by a traditional code that kept them from using the weapons of the enemy. As a price of victory, however, the Snopeses had to serve the mechanized civilization of the North, which was morally impotent in itself, but which, with the aid of its Southern retainers, ended by corrupting the Southern nation.

Faulkner's novels of contemporary Southern life continue the legend into a period that he regards as one of moral confusion and social decay. He is continually seeking in them for violent images to convey his sense of despair. . . .

In all his novels dealing with the present, Faulkner makes it clear that the descendants of the old ruling caste have the wish but not the courage or the strength to prevent this new disaster. . . . Faulkner's novels are full of well-meaning and even admirable persons, not only the grandsons of the cotton aristocracy, but also pine-hill farmers and storekeepers and sewing-machine agents and Negro cooks and sharecroppers; but they are almost all of them defeated by circumstances and they carry with them a sense of their own doom.

They also carry, whether heroes or villains, a curious sense of submission to their fate. "There is not one of Faulkner's characters," says André Gide in his dialogue on "The New American Novelists," "who properly speaking, has a soul"; and I think he means that not one of them exercises the faculty of conscious choice between good and evil. They are haunted, obsessed, driven forward by some inner necessity. Like Miss Rosa Coldfield, in *Absalom, Absalom!* they exist in "that dream state in which you run without moving from a terror in which you cannot believe, toward a safety in which you have no faith.". . .

Even when they seem to be guided by a conscious purpose, like Colonel Sutpen, it is not something they have chosen by an act of will, but something that has taken possession of them: Sutpen's great design was "not what he wanted to do but what he just had to do, had to do it whether he wanted to or not, because if he did not do it he knew that he could never live with himself for the rest of his life."

# *Absalom, Absalom!* as an Epic Novel

James H. Justus

James H. Justus argues that William Faulkner's *Absalom, Absalom!* is best read as an epic, in large part because Thomas Sutpen is a character of heroic proportion. Justus concludes that Sutpen is a demi-god flawed by pride, lack of self-awareness, and lack of scruples. James H. Justus has contributed critical articles to scholarly journals and written *The Achievements of Robert Penn Warren.*

I would suggest that *Absalom, Absalom!* be read as epic. It is the one genre that equals and even surpasses tragedy in dignity and grandeur. It is no less artistic than tragedy in its selection of incident, though that selection is determined by different impulses. . . .

[Epic as narrative fiction] would exclude clear-cut pieces of drama and would retain all the other associations: characters of high position engaged in a series of adventures, organic narrative revolving about a central figure of heroic proportions, action important to a nation or a race at a specific point in its development, and a style that is dignified, majestic, and elevated. Such is the minimum boundary within which the term operates; in addition, certain secondary characteristics emerge as common and proper to epic.

There is much to indicate that *Absalom* occupies a rather special position in the Yoknapatawpha saga. . . . The fall of the House of Sutpen is accompanied by a fully conscious analysis of the evil effects of that family on its own members and on the immediate community, on the South, and by extension on the nation and the world at large. The technical virtuosity of *The Sound and the Fury* should not obscure the fact that *Absalom, Absalom! is* the more ambitious work.

Faulkner lavishes on Sutpen the most detailed and the

Excerpted from "The Epic Design of *Absalom, Absalom!*" by James H. Justus, *Texas Studies in Literature and Language,* vol. 4 (Summer 1962), pp. 157–76. Published by the University of Texas Press. Copyright 1962. Reprinted by permission of the publisher.

most careful filling-in of any of his characters; it is as if he alone of all the Faulkner characters were meant to be full-scale, to possess in full what Quentin, Bayard Sartoris, Jewel Bundren, Joe Christmas, and a half-dozen others possess in part. In no other novel is there so much energy devoted to the characterization of one man; no single point of view (not even the one direct-three refracted techniques of *The Sound and the Fury*) can possibly explain Sutpen: his very substance depends on a pooling of impressions by three and sometimes four or five different people. And when all this is done, he remains mythic, as if even the legend that he generates in the county cannot wholly apprehend him. In no other novel is Faulkner so consciously aware of history as history, of not only recounting the facts and quasi facts of history but also of attempting to order them, to understand them, to ask *why?* And in no other novel is there so unambiguous an answer. Because of the monumental task, the process of getting to the answer results in an agony of style far more heightened than that in his other novels. I am reading *Absalom, Absalom!* as epic, then, because no other reading can so fully explain its height and breadth. . . .

The heroic stature of Thomas Sutpen is measured in terms of his compulsion, an obsessive plan for founding a dynasty at whatever cost. The cost is heavy, and the dynasty comes to nothing; but between the wrenching of Sutpen's Hundred out of the swamps and the escape of his great-grandson, the idiot Jim Bond, the acts of Sutpen are impressive. That these acts are demonic is not to be denied, but it is a misplaced dependence upon Rosa Coldfield's narration to conclude that Sutpen is in fact a "demon" or that he is wholly a "villain."

## ROSA COLDFIELD'S VIEW OF SUTPEN

The demonic element in Sutpen is inherent in his compulsion, and the term can in varying degrees apply to the entire range of characters who are repeatedly, from all points of view, called "ghosts." Some are doomed and some are damned; all are "invoked" and the entire legend is "recapitulation evoked." It is not accidental that the frame scenes are drenched with atmosphere common to the invoking ritual—the overall frame itself is a cold, tomblike sitting room at Harvard in late evening, and the subframes are a "dim hot airless room" in the "long still hot weary dead September afternoon"; a front gallery quiet and hushed in the wisteria twilight; a buggy at night leading to a house inhabited by ghosts both dead and alive; a swamp campsite guarded by naked, wild Negroes. And the ghosts so invoked do attain a kind of permanence, at least long enough to play out their legend again for meaning-seeking Quentin. Rosa's "this demon" becomes itself "enclosed by its effluvium of hell, its aura of unregeneration," and "ogre-shape" and "djinn,"[1] and "the evil's source and head" outlasting most of its victims. But in her railing, self-pitying moments, Rosa momentarily forgets the "ogre" as the forty-three-year-old object of her pure hate, and even allows herself respect for Sutpen, his energy, and stern self-consistency. There is that moment when the three women sit at the mansion waiting for him to return from the war:

> We talked of him . . . of what he would do: how begin the Herculean task which we knew he would set himself, into which . . . he would undoubtedly sweep us with the old ruthlessness whether we would or no.

And to this respect is added, in small measure, a touch of pity that she can pass on to someone other than herself. This strange mixture of respect and pity is most obvious when she is describing the "old man's solitary fury" as he dismisses the Ku Klux Klan delegation, the symbol of the "changed new time" which Sutpen fights "as though he were trying to dam a river with his bare hands and a shingle." Even in Rosa's version Sutpen attains something out of the mythic mold, of man's struggle to order his world, even when it is crumbling and even when most of its collapse is attributable to his own pride.

## THE COMPSONS' VERSION OF SUTPEN

The "demon" Sutpen is even more modified by Mr. Compson's (and his father's) version of the story. Here the key is the more human one of "ambition." The phrases that come to characterize Sutpen in these versions are "gaunt and tireless driving, that conviction for haste and of fleeing time," "grim and unflagging fury," "watchfulness" that only sporadically turns to "braggadocio or belligerence"—he becomes, in short, "the slave of his secret and furious impa-

---

1. also jinni. In Muslim legend, a spirit capable of assuming human or animal form and exercising supernatural influence over people.

tience." He is the spiritual solitary who, frustrated in his first attempts to build his design in an alien land, without bitterness but with honed haste makes his second attempt in an equally alien land. The power he wields comes not in fact from an alliance with the underworld (though certainly with the permissive detachment of providence and the natural world), but from an attenuated faith in himself. Mr. Compson remembers his father's impression: "Given the occasion and the need, this man can and will do anything." Sutpen says that during his brief sojourn in the West Indies he learned that any man could get rich if he could boast cleverness and courage: "the latter of which I believed that I possessed, the former of which I believed that . . . I should learn." And his Mississippi venture, Mr. Compson surmises, he takes seriously, watchfully, with

> that unsleeping care which must have known that it could permit itself but one mistake; that alertness for measuring and weighing event against eventuality, circumstance against human nature, his own fallible judgment and mortal clay against not only human but natural forces, choosing and discarding, compromising with his dream and his ambition.

The emphasis here is clear: Sutpen is mortal, he is fallible, he is a compromiser. Whatever element of superhumanity is generated by his legend, it comes from Sutpen's own knowledge of his needs and methods for accomplishing them. He becomes the self-made man in its apotheosis.

### FAULKNER'S VERSION OF SUTPEN

Here lies Faulkner's version of the epic hero—perhaps the only version a modern American writer could bring to life. It is only as the pieces of the legend are fitted together that Sutpen's weaknesses as self-made hero are allowed to enter the story. Our first vision of him, without the later undercutting, is at least one continuing strand of the legend—the communal attitude of Jefferson:

> Immobile, bearded and hand palm-lifted the horseman sat; behind him the wild blacks and the captive architect huddled quietly, carrying in bloodless paradox the shovels and picks and axes of peaceful conquest. Then in the long unamaze Quentin seemed to watch them overrun suddenly the hundred square miles of tranquil and astonished earth and drag house and formal gardens violently out of the soundless Nothing and clap them down like cards upon a table beneath the up-palm immobile and pontific, creating the Sutpen's Hundred, the *Be Sutpen's Hundred* like the oldtime *Be Light*.

He is a composite Achilles-Aeneas-Agamemnon—and more: he is God Himself. This incredible picture, in terms of a painting, an etching, or a frieze, is a powerful stimulant for the community; it is only with the most severe diminution— much later—that the picture is blurred. And we may be sure that for many in Jefferson the picture is never really blurred.

## QUENTIN'S AND SHREVE'S IMAGES OF SUTPEN

Still another Sutpen emerges from the imaginary reconstruction by Quentin and Shreve; with partial understanding Shreve whimsically echoes Rosa's "demon" Sutpen, but in an obvious attempt to clarify this view, the two students call forth an entire cluster of epithets and metaphors that will come closer to striking the truth of Sutpen: "this Faustus, this demon, this Beelzebub" escaping his harried Creditor, hoping with "outrageous bravado" to fool the Creditor by the illusion that "time had not elapsed." They even imagine Sutpen more an "ancient stiff-jointed Pyramus" than a "widowed Agamemnon," a "mad impotent old man" seeing himself as the "old wornout cannon which realizes that it can deliver just one more fierce shot and crumble to dust in its own furious blast and recoil."

The perplexed images of Sutpen reach their height in Chapter VI, where these youthful minds sit through all the stories looking for a complete image. Appropriately, this is the only version which asks questions of itself. The other views, while partial, are products of long-consolidated musing: whether outraged, bemused, or comprehending, they each offer the fragmented Sutpen to Quentin and Shreve with an assurance that excludes the necessity for further questions.

## SUTPEN'S LACK OF SELF-KNOWLEDGE

But Sutpen's own story, transmitted through Quentin's grandfather, not only gives the legendary figure a history; it also opens up an important area of his nature—his justness— which proves to be the most elusive of his qualities and the one most violently rejected by the narrators. Sutpen's original repudiation, the sin that is to reverberate all the way through the stark mansion halls to 1910, is in his terms not so much a consciously immoral act as a satisfactory legal arrangement. It is his innocence, of course, that can see such a momentous act in those terms; and, though our realization of this does not neutralize the wrong act, it does almost eliminate the much touted demonic, consciously villainous side of his nature.

## SUTPEN MANIFESTS HIS IGNORANCE

After this, his own version, he stands as an unfortunate creature without self-knowledge, without even knowing he needs self-knowledge. Apparently there is no advance in moral mastery of himself from the night of the architect-hunt (when he related the first part of his story to Quentin's grandfather) to the time in General Compson's office thirty years later (when he tells the second part). There is only a puzzled calm, as if he "had long since given up any hope of understanding" what went wrong with his design. There is no evidence in this section that the repudiation of a wife and child cursed Sutpen's conscience; his innocence, his trust in his own brand of rationality, told him what old General Compson had to admit was "a good and valid claim"—that because he entered into a marriage "in good faith, with no reservations as to his obscure origin and material equipment," he could dissolve that marriage when he discovered in his wife "not only reservation but actual misrepresentation."

The act of taking only twenty Negroes from all that he might have taken—when he voluntarily relinquished the first design in Haiti—had both "legal and moral sanction even if not the delicate one of conscience." When judgment is injected into this account, it comes not from the grandfather (at least not directly), but from Quentin, who with no little tone of exasperation, defines that special kind of Sutpenism: "that innocence which believed that the ingredients of morality were like the ingredients of pie or cake and once you had measured them and balanced them and mixed them and put them into the oven it was all finished and nothing but pie or cake could come out." But to Sutpen, his own behavior is just:

> I made no attempt to keep not only that which I might consider myself to have earned at the risk of my life but which had been given to me by signed testimonials, but on the contrary I declined and resigned all right and claim to this in order that I might repair whatever injustice I might be considered to have done by so providing for the two persons whom I might be considered to have deprived of anything I might later possess: and this was agreed to, mind; agreed to between the two parties.

This legalistic morality does not take away the recognition that a deeper morality is needed, but it does take away the "monstrousness" of the act. And it is further alleviated when (according to Shreve and Quentin) the cast-off wife enters into a vicious and revengeful "design" of her own to destroy Sutpen's. Further, the very quality of Sutpen's speech is as indicative of his strengths as of his radical weaknesses. Our distaste for the self-conscious, florid bombast derived from books and the swaggering painfully learned is considerably lessened as it filters through this perpetual and clinging innocence. (This brilliant suspension of characteristics is not unlike Fitzgerald's Jay Gatsby, whose own innocence and perplexity go far in neutralizing his vulgar commitment to success.)

## WASH JONES'S VIEW OF SUTPEN

There is nothing of regret or even frustration when Sutpen rides off to war; rather, it is another gesture apparently confirming himself in his belief that he possessed something that caused "destiny to shape itself to him like his clothes did," a destiny that "fitted itself to him, to his innocence, his pristine aptitude for platform drama and childlike heroic simplicity." And it is in this particular role that he achieves full heroic stature in the eyes of Wash Jones, who sees him as a "fine proud man." He speculates that if "God Himself was to come down and ride the natural earth, that's what He would aim to look like." And just before his final and only disillusionment, Wash indulges himself in a sincere panegyric:[2]

> He is bigger than all them Yankees that killed us and ourn, that killed his wife and widowed his daughter and druv his son from home, that stole his niggers and ruined his land; bigger than this whole county that he fit for and in payment for which has brung him to keeping a little country store for his bread and meat; bigger than the scorn and denial which hit helt to his lips like the bitter cup in the Book. And how could I have lived nigh to him for twenty years without being touched and changed by him? Maybe I am not as big as he is and maybe I did not do any of the galloping. But at least I was drug along where he went. And me and him can still do hit and will ever so, if so be he will show me what he aims for me to do.

There is no evidence to support Quentin and Shreve's idea that Wash saw through the shabby pretensions of the coun-

2. elaborate praise

try storekeeper or that he saw him as a "furious lecherous wreck." As he has faith in the heroic figure who once galloped about on a black thoroughbred, so he has faith that that hero's association with his granddaughter will turn out honorably. Mr. Compson explains the reason for such a faith when he says that Wash's morality was "a good deal like Sutpen's, that told him he was right in the face of all fact and usage and everything else." Certainly Wash's attitude toward Sutpen, coming as it does in Sutpen's inglorious years, cannot be ignored. The glory of both his character and his accomplishments trails horizontally all the way from the battlefields to the crossroads store and vertically all through the layers of acceptance and faith up to the very moment of murder and suicide.

## THE SIMPLICITY AND COMPLEXITY OF SUTPEN

Sutpen's refusal to recognize Bon is again a failure in morality; it is not, however, a question of hate, either personal (for Bon as "avenging" son) or impersonal (for Bon as the vessel of mingled blood). It is not a question of love, for there is little evidence to suppose Sutpen felt love for any of his children or either of his wives. It is a question of his amoral rationality— that cool assessment of what would and what would not be "adjunctive or incremental" to his design. In a very real sense, then, there is strength as well as weakness in Sutpen's consistency and singlemindedness. He is wrong, but he is impressive. His isolation carries with it an imperious air throughout all his relationships with others—his solitary fact-finding trip to New Orleans, his arch wedding ceremony with Ellen, and aloof hospitality to the community in the half-finished mansion, his curt dismissal of the Klan delegation. Even his most impious acts have an air of stolid impersonality; his very obduracy is removed from the brunt of human passions and elevated to a peak of disinterested immunity.

Because of the nature of the narrators, it is easy to forget the admirable qualities of Sutpen: his refusal to accept neighborly favors when he cannot return them, his practical demonstrations of superiority over his slaves by sportsmanlike contests, his steadfast though puzzled search for personal fault rather than the easier act of blaming fate. Sutpen's fall is the death and dismemberment of the demigod, and if he cannot command his own reassembling and resurrection, there are plenty of ordinary mortals who gladly confer immortality on him by rising to sing of his glory. But, however strenuously invoked, his summoning remains partial; though he is declared in "this shadowy attenuation of time" to be "possessing now heroic proportions," he still hovers "shadowy, inscrutable and serene"—a satisfactory state for Mr. Compson, who as a sentimental, bemused cynic is more comfortable with these figures as ghosts. Mr. Compson recognizes that the indulgent pleasure he gets in invoking these shades can never be equaled by a complete comprehension of the legend. He takes refuge in contrasting the unheroic present with the heroic past with all its legendary attributes: "not dwarfed and involved but distinct, uncomplex" people who had "the gift of living once or dying once instead of being diffused and scattered creatures."

## DESPITE COMPSON'S NARRATION, SUTPEN IS HEROIC

Mr. Compson contributes not a little to the wormy tone of this story. Defeated himself, he revels in the principle of Fate, which he characterizes as the grim equalizer of all ambition and assertion of human will. From no other narrator do we get so much romanticized glorification of Fate. It is not surprising that he salutes the Sutpens as heroic. As long as their defeat is so luxuriantly sung, the futile effort for victory itself is worth a chorus or two. Both are of a single piece: if seeing Fate, doom, and a general curse as an answer for the Sutpen fall is easy, seeing the grand resistance to those inexorables is even easier. What is to Faulkner's credit is that something of heroic dimensions is visible when we cut through the Compson personality. Perhaps the undercutting by an easy cynicism strengthens the heroic image of Sutpen, for what does remain is earned (just as in Rosa's account) and, with all views assimilated, remarkably substantial for a ghost in a legend. . . .

A reading of *Absalom, Absalom!* as epic, then, does not necessitate a rigid categorization, for certainly many traditional aspects of epic as a specialized genre will not be found in Faulkner's novel. Nor should they be. . . . The story is narrated, and the narrator is both a public voice as well as Quentin Compson, the morbid, too-sensitive suicide-to-be. No other major novel in the series posits an action, a theme, on so high an eminence and on so broad an expanse. Nor does any other of the Yoknapatawpha novels attempt a full-scale characterization of such scope with all the attendant legendary attributes of a mythic hero dominating that action or illustrating that theme. For these reasons it seems mandatory that we reject any attempt to read *Absalom, Absalom!* minimally; its "category" must be sufficiently flexible and inclusive so that it will not only incorporate minimal readings but also consolidate and transmute them under its governing design. The design that comes closest to achieving this is the epic.

# The Structure of
# *Go Down, Moses*

Lyall H. Powers

Lyall H. Powers discusses the seven stories in William Faulkner's *Go Down, Moses* into three parts. Three stories in part one reveal the heritage of the McCaslin family; in part two three stories concern Isaac McCaslin's discovery of that heritage. Finally, in part three, one story involves hope that the racial oppression inherent in the family and the culture will one day change. Powers identifies Faulkner's broad theme as respect and love for all of God's creation and the courage to act responsibly on its behalf. Though Ike McCaslin understands respect and love, he lacks the third virtue, courage; instead, hope lies in Lucas Beauchamp, who possesses all three virtues. Lyall H. Powers has taught at the universities of Wisconsin, Michigan, British Columbia, and Hawaii. He is the author of eight books on American author Henry James and editor of numerous books.

*Go Down, Moses* (1942) occupies a special place among Faulkner's important works. One part of it, "The Bear," is not only his best known piece of fiction but also the one that has elicited the most critical commentary. The frame of specific temporal reference is further extended here than in all of his other major fiction. Following the familiar practice of the first dozen years or so of the Yoknapatawpha Saga—that of doubling back over ground already crossed in order to discover and examine the antecedent cause of the growing evil already exposed—Faulkner has in *Go Down, Moses* gone furthest into his characters' history, to the virtual discovery of the New World; yet this novel bursts into our own time, into the middle years (appropriately) of the Second World War. While much has been settled, fictionally, by *Go Down,*

Excerpted from *Faulkner's Yoknapatawpha Comedy* by Lyall H. Powers (Ann Arbor: University of Michigan Press, 1980). Copyright ©1980 by The University of Michigan Press. Reprinted by permission of the publisher.

*Moses* and by the critical commentary it has received, a close rereading of the novel will reveal certain unanswered questions and unresolved difficulties. Those answers and resolutions can best be found in our rereading by attending to the nature of the novel's focus on Isaac McCaslin—surely the Moses of the novel's title—and by looking closely at his role and its implications for this land of ours where a "Pharaoh" takes precedence over a King.

Mr. Cleanth Brooks has made the interesting suggestion that *Go Down, Moses* might have been more usefully entitled *The McCaslins,* "for the book has to do with the varying fortunes of that family." I would modify that suggestion only to emphasize that the book has to do with Ike's understanding of and finally his contribution to the fortunes of that family. The crucial question facing Isaac McCaslin is "What does it mean to be one of the family?" In terms of the novel's metaphor, the family is, of course, the McCaslins; in terms of the broadest significance of that metaphor, however, the family is the human family. To answer such a crucial question, one must know and understand the family heritage—must recognize the virtues and the source of goodness whence they derive, as well as the sins and the source of evil which promotes them; one must also understand what has been and what now can be done to foster the former and combat the latter. In dealing with this question and the problem of answering it satisfactorily, Faulkner has offered a combination of dramatic expression and discursive narration in the various pieces which make up *Go Down, Moses.*

The novel is clearly enough Isaac's from the opening lines onward. Yet the beginning statement about "Uncle Ike" is left suspended, to be finished later. And that is, I think, the initial clue to the novel's three-part structure. The first three stories ("Was," "The Fire and the Hearth," and "Pantaloon in Black") portray Isaac's heritage; this permits us an objective view of the features, the good and the evil, which characterize his heritage, and allows us to make our balanced judgment of it. The second part ("The Old People," "The Bear," and "Delta Autumn") presents us with Isaac's discovery of that heritage, his education in its good and evil. We not only have his experiences but are privy to his thoughts about those crucial experiences. Since we already know, from reading the first part, what Isaac must learn, we can better sympathize with him as he discovers—sees and defines for

himself—the good of the wilderness and the evil of exploitation; and, more important, we can judge the decisions he
subsequently makes on the basis of his understanding of his
heritage. The first part shows the scene upon which Ike will
enter; the second shows us Ike's reaction to that scene. The
third part ("Go Down, Moses") serves as the conclusion,
which not only rounds off the action of the novel but also
points ahead to the consequences which will follow from
Ike's experience and his reaction to it.

The virtues discovered in *Go Down, Moses* are, most simply expressed, respect and love for God's creation and the
courage to accept the responsibility which that respect and
love demand. The source of goodness whence those virtues
spring is God's creation itself, or, more properly, right
knowledge of God's creation. The sins and wickedness discovered in the novel are, of course, the opposite of that—lack
of respect and love, or failure of courage when some respect
and love have been awakened.

## STORIES OF THE MCCASLIN HERITAGE

We are led gently into the heart of the matter by the initial
"Was." The hearty joviality and lusty romp may easily cam-
ouflage the more serious concerns of the story. . . . The awful
fact of the condition of slavery is muffled under a chuckle,
but it is there. Similarly, in the Beauchamp hyperbole at
Warwick, the miserable code which depends upon the institution of slavery for its support and sustenance—the exclusive, introverted, and gentle code of the pseudoaristocratic
way of "the Old South," the "Southern gentleman," and the
"Southern Belle"—holds sway.

"Was" has opened the story of the McCaslin heritage *in me-
dias res.* Our attention is directed to an episode in the life of
the middle generation of McCaslins—the twin sons of old
Carothers McCaslin, first of that name in Yoknapatawpha
County, and the father and uncle of Isaac McCaslin, last of
that name (legitimately) in Yoknapatawpha County. "The Fire
and the Hearth" is concerned with two other branches—the
white Edmondses, descended from the distaff[1] side, and the
black Beauchamps, descended from old Carothers Mc-
Caslin's left hand. Three closely related features of the novel's
principal concern emerge strongly in this story: proper re-

1. mother's

spect for the land, love, and the responsible courage to sustain that respect and love. . . .

Lucas [Beauchamp] is and has been the man he claims to be. He has the necessary virtues of respect for God's creatures and of love, and he has likewise the courage to accept the responsibility for what he rightly respects and loves. This discovery of human virtue in the son of Tomey's Turl, whose pursuit we were invited to laugh at and whom we were permitted to dismiss as a rather shrewd but inhuman clown (in "Was"), comes as a bracing contrast.

In the subsequent story, "Pantaloon in Black," one aspect of Lucas's life gains special emphasis by the illumination reflected from the profoundly pathetic love of Rider and Mannie. The association of that young couple of newlyweds, so soon separated by death, with Lucas and Molly is made quite specific: "they married and he [Rider] rented the cabin from Carothers Edmonds and built a fire on the hearth on their wedding night as the tale told how Uncle Lucas Beauchamp . . . had done on his forty-five years ago and

---

### IKE'S LACK OF COURAGE

*Ike McCaslin fails to act on behalf of God's creatures when he does not help a pregnant young woman who comes to his hunting camp. In the excerpt from the end of "Delta Autumn," Ike keenly understands virtue and wickedness, but he chooses to draw the blankets around him and avoid responsibility.*

"Old man," she said, "have you lived so long and forgotten so much that you dont remember anything you ever knew or felt or even heard about love?"

Then she was gone too. The waft of light and the murmur of the constant rain flowed into the tent and then out again as the flap fell. Lying back once more, trembling, panting, the blanket huddled to his chin and his hands crossed on his breast, he listened to the pop and snarl, the mounting then fading whine of the motor until it died away and once again the tent held only silence and the sound of rain. And cold too: he lay shaking faintly and steadily in it, rigid save for the shaking. This Delta, he thought: This Delta. *This land which man has deswamped and denuded and derivered in two generations so that white men can own plantations and commute every night to Memphis and black men own plantations and ride in jim crow cars to Chicago to live in millionaires' man-*

which had burned ever since. . . ."

This first section of three stories presents quite clearly enough those sins of disrespect for and hence exploitation of the land and of human beings which are regularly the basic concern of Faulkner's fiction. And in the character of Lucas Beauchamp we find embodied the virtues of respect for the land and people, of generous and effective human love, and of stoutly courageous responsibility. A tragic qualification is that because of the peculiar institution which restricts Lucas's field of influence—that way of life which, Faulkner's work persuades us, was responsible for the demise of the old South and prevents the successful rise of a new South, and a new North too—his virtues cannot effect all the good they otherwise might.

### Isaac McCaslin Discovers His Heritage

The next group of three stories presents the same heinous sins as Ike McCaslin discovers them—discovers them to

*sions on Lakeshore Drive, where white men rent farms and live like niggers and niggers crop on shares and live like animals, where cotton is planted and grows man-tall in the very cracks of the sidewalks, and usury and mortgage and bankruptcy and measureless wealth, Chinese and African and Aryan and Jew, all breed and spawn together until no man has time to say which one is which nor cares.* . . . No wonder the ruined woods I used to know dont cry for retribution! he thought: The people who have destroyed it will accomplish its revenge.

The tent flap jerked rapidly in and fell. He did not move save to turn his head and open his eyes. It was Legate. . . .

"Looking for Roth's knife," Legate said. "I come back to get a horse. We got a deer on the ground.". . .

"Wait," McCaslin said. He moved, suddenly, onto his elbow. "What was it?" Legate paused for an instant beneath the lifted flap. He did not look back.

"Just a deer, Uncle Ike," he said impatiently. "Nothing extra." He was gone; again the flap fell behind him, wafting out of the tent again the faint light and the constant and grieving rain. McCaslin lay back down, the blanket once more drawn to his chin, his crossed hands once more weightless on his breast in the empty tent.

"It was a doe," he said.

have existed even among the aborigines of this brave New World of ours—and the stories also show us Ike discovering the virtues necessary to combat those sins. And in the scope of these stories we also see the tragic failure of one so enlightened to act on his knowledge.

"The Old People" is best seen as the immediate preparation for the important discoveries Isaac will make in "The Bear." It is Isaac's story (as indeed the whole novel is)—the story of "his maturing, of that for which Sam had been training him all his life some day to dedicate himself." And it is about the shooting of a buck when Ike is twelve—or, rather, the shooting of two bucks. After Ike successfully shot his first buck, Sam Fathers marked him with its hot blood, as a ritual of initiation into the mystery of the hunters. . . .

The second stage of Isaac's initiation is given much fuller development in "The Bear." To begin with, the story gives us to understand that Ike is being prepared to enter the mystery of the hunters, whose life in the wilderness is guided by certain rituals of behavior and whose role as hunters demands certain qualities in the men themselves. When Ike has evidently proved to Sam Fathers's satisfaction that he possesses (at least potentially) those necessary qualities—honor and pride and pity and courage and love—he is given the final test of self-reliance. He must strip himself of the last aids of civilization, watch and compass and gun, and face the wilderness on his own. When he does so, he is granted his first vision of Ben, the bear. Like the magnificent buck in "The Old People," Ben does not come into view, he just suddenly materializes:

> . . . he saw the bear. It did not emerge, appear: it was just there, immobile, fixed in the green and windless noon's hot dappling . . . looking at him. . . . Then it was gone. It didn't walk into the woods. It faded, sank back into the wilderness without motion.

Ike has thus become one of the family of hunters, has entered the mystery of the hunters' fraternity. . . .

"Delta Autumn" refers again and quite specifically to Ike's relationship with his wife and establishes clearly the connection between his failure of love and his failure of courage which prompted his repudiation of the McCaslin inheritance. Old Uncle Ike reviews his long life, from the beginning of his initiation at the hands of Sam Fathers, through the decision which brought him to where he is—"past seventy and nearer eighty than he ever corroborated any more, a widower now and uncle to half a county and father to no one," as the opening lines of the novel had told us. . . .

The last word on this important characterization of Ike McCaslin is provided by the young woman who appears at the hunting camp carrying Roth Edmonds's baby. Ike gives her the money Roth has left for her and urges her to leave. . . . Then she is gone, and old Uncle Ike, father to no one, returns to the comfort of his cocoon; he lies down again in bed and draws the blanket up to his chin, hugging to himself— whether he fully recognizes it yet or not—his impotent self-righteousness.

It is quite true, of course, that Isaac has clearly seen and properly identified the evil which has made the McCaslin land a cursed heritage; and we would do wrong to take from Ike credit for that clearsightedness. It is with his decision about what to do with that cursed heritage, however, that we must be most alertly concerned. And we must recognize the extent to which Faulkner has gone in expressing Ike's failure of courage and love as the reason for that decision. . . .

## THE SIGNIFICANCE OF IKE MCCASLIN'S FAILURE

To a considerable extent, Faulkner's use of the Theme of the Second Chance sharpens our grief and the tragic import of Ike's failure. Typically, the theme shows us not simply the repetition of misdoing, of the denial of Good, but within that repetition the opportunity to compensate for the earlier failure. And, as is most appropriate, the Second Chance is presented in terms of Love—the opportunity for Love. . . . We and Ike observe the Second Chance offered and refused, and Ike enacts that refusal himself. . . .

Much of the tragic impact of Isaac's failure derives from the fact that he knows—and quite clearly at his best moments—just what he is doing, just exactly how he is being apostate from what Sam Fathers had taught him. We have seen his flat refusal to be "an Isaac born into a later life than Abraham's" and the reason for that refusal. . . . He does know, and at such moments can almost judge himself honestly for what he is. The fact of that self-knowledge both mitigates and aggravates our sense of Ike's tragic failure. That he knows what is right to do and yet cannot do it gives rise to pity for his case; that he willfully fails to do the right, yet hypocritically rolls on his tongue forever the rhetoric of righteousness, gives rise to the terror. The tragic effect is there. . . .

## No Change in the Status Quo: "Not Now! Not Yet!"

We are left, then, with the brief third part of *Go Down, Moses*—the concluding story. Its title has the effect of a plaintive reiteration of the urgent admonition of the novel's title: go down, Moses. . . . The ostensible Moses, Isaac Mc-Caslin, has thoroughly failed to heed that request, as we have seen. His role in "Go Down, Moses" is assumed by Gavin Stevens; and we might consider that here is the offer of a Second Chance, that perhaps a "Moses" with the necessary qualifications will now appear and that God's people—of whatever complexion—will be set free. We learn little about Gavin in this final story, only the essential fact that he will fail, as Isaac failed, by doing his bit . . . to maintain the status quo. . . .

As usual in Faulkner's presentation of the "tragedy" of his good, weak hero, we find the cause of failure here carefully defined and the possibility of other options clearly expressed. In other words, in *Go Down, Moses* as in traditional tragic drama, we understand why this particular hero has failed and how he—and indeed we—might avoid that tragic failure. The effect is pitiable and terrible, to be sure, but by no means desperate; it is, in its way, hopeful, positive, instructive. To augment that effect Faulkner has relied upon another character—potentially one of the Saving Remnant—who possesses precisely those qualities the lack of which fostered Isaac McCaslin's failure. Lucas Beauchamp is presented, particularly in "The Fire and the Hearth," as capable of the love so sadly lacking in Ike. His courage in standing up to those who have wronged him specifically and generally is far beyond any demanded of Ike; and his responsibility in caring for his own is just exactly that which Isaac—for all his righteous rhetoric—flatly refuses. Furthermore, the basis for his accepting what Ike at every turn refuses is just that attitude toward the fact of mutability and mortality which Ike cannot bring himself—for all of Sam's careful instruction—to accept. By means of some few impressive touches, the novel encourages comparison between Lucas and Sam, and, perhaps even more significant, between Lucas and Ben. Like Sam, he is victimized by the white blood in his veins; yet, by every action, he expresses the fact that his problem is not servitude but bondage: his soul is distinctly his own. Like old Ben, Lucas has the fierce and ruthless pride of liberty and freedom and the fierce and ruthless desire for life that can see those cherished features threatened fearlessly and almost with joy, seeming deliberately to put them into jeopardy the better to savor them. Lucas apparently knows—as Sam wished Isaac to learn—that while the body dies, the body's beauty lives. Consequently, Lucas is not afraid of life and its demands, but bravely and lovingly affirms them. And Isaac was more correct than he knew in asserting that characters like Lucas will "endure." The novel also strongly expresses the idea that Lucas, or rather the "beauty" that Lucas embodies, will live, that it is free of mere carnal mortality. . . .

Although both Lucas and Isaac are absent from this final piece of the novel, the difference in effect of the two absences is impressive. We have seen what is virtually the end of Isaac as he wraps himself up in his comforting blanket at the end of "Delta Autumn." To all intents and purposes, Isaac is finished. Lucas has not been at all accounted for in this way. He is, then, conspicuous by his absence, since, once again, the acute need for those virtues he possesses is stridently expressed by the action of Isaac's replacement. And again it is Lucas's family which needs the benefit of his virtues. In a sense, Lucas would be the successful Moses to which the novel's title addresses its urgent appeal. The very conditions of the society in which he is granted an unequal share make it impossible for him to fulfill that broadly liberating function. His potential is not recognized, or, in Isaac's mournful refrain, not now! not yet!

# Race as a Theme in
# *Go Down, Moses*

Lionel Trilling

Lionel Trilling criticizes the complex style and entanglement of characters in William Faulkner's *Go Down, Moses*, but praises the book as a convincing exposé of racism in the South. According to Trilling, the Edmonds family represents southern tradition, while Isaac McCaslin represents freedom and nature. Trilling cites Faulkner's focus on sexual and blood relations as a complicating factor in black-white conflicts. Influential critic Lionel Trilling taught English at Columbia University in New York City. He is the author of *Matthew Arnold*, *The Liberal Imagination*, *The Opposing Self*, and the novel *The Middle of the Journey*.

William Faulkner's [*Go Down, Moses*] is brought out as a collection of stories, but six of the seven stories deal with a single theme, the relation of the Mississippi McCaslins to the Negroes about them, and they have a coherence strong enough to constitute, if not exactly a novel, then at least a narrative which begins, develops, and concludes. The seventh and alien story, 'Pantaloon in Black', is inferior both in conception and in execution; why it was placed in the midst of the others is hard to understand, for it diminishes their coherence. But conceivably Mr. Faulkner intended it to do just that, wishing to exempt the collection from being taken for a novel and judged as such. Yet it is only as an integrated work that the group of McCaslin stories can be read.

Mr. Faulkner's literary mannerisms are somewhat less obtrusive than they have been, but they are still dominant in his writing, and to me they are faults. For one thing, I find tiresome Mr. Faulkner's reliance on the method of memory to tell his stories. No doubt we can accept what so many

From Lionel Trilling, "The McCaslins of Mississippi," *Nation*, May 30, 1942. Reprinted by permission of the *Nation* magazine.

Southern novelists imply, that in the South a continuous
acute awareness of regional, local, and family history is one
of the conditions of thought. But the prose in which Mr.
Faulkner renders this element of his stories is, to me, most
irritating; it drones so lyrically on its way, so intentionally
losing its syntax in its long sentences, so full of self-pity expressed through somniloquism[1] or ventriloquism. Then, too,
while I am sure that prose fiction may make great demands
on our attention, it ought not to make these demands arbitrarily, and there is no reason why Mr. Faulkner cannot set-
tle to whom the pronoun 'he' refers. Mr. Faulkner's book is
worth effort but not, I think, the kind of effort which I found
necessary: I had to read it twice to get clear not only the
finer shades of meaning but the simple primary intentions,
and I had to construct an elaborate genealogical table to understand the family connections.

## THE COMPLEX RACIAL ISSUE

These considerations aside, Mr. Faulkner's book is in many
ways admirable. The six McCaslin stories are temperate and
passionate, and they suggest more convincingly than anything I have read the complex tragedy of the South's racial
dilemma. The first of the stories is set in 1856; it is the humorous tale of the chase after the runaway Tomey's Turl—it
takes a certain effort to make sure that this is a slave, not a
dog—of how old Buck McCaslin is trapped into marriage by
Miss Sophonsiba Beauchamp and her brother Hubert (right-
fully the Earl of Warwick), and of the poker game that is
played for Tomey's Turl; the humor is abated when we learn
that Turl is half-brother to one of the poker players. The last
story is set in 1940; its central figure is the Negro murderer
Samuel Worsham Beauchamp, descendant of Tomey's Turl
and related to the McCaslins through more lines than one.

The best of the book does not deal directly with the Negro
fate but with the spiritual condition of the white men who
have that fate at their disposal. The Edmonds branch of the
McCaslin family—there are three generations of Edmonds,
but Mr. Faulkner likes to telescope the generations and all
the Edmondses are really the same person: this does not exactly make for clarity—represents the traditional South;
Isaac McCaslin, who is by way of being the hero of the nar-

1. talking in one's sleep

rative, represents the way of regeneration. The Edmondses are shown as being far from bad; in their relation to their Negroes they are often generous, never brutal, scarcely even irresponsible; but they accept their tradition and act upon their superiority and their rights, and the result is tragedy and degeneration both for the Negroes and for themselves. The effects are not always immediate and obvious; one of the best passages in the book, and one of the most crucial, is that in which, as a boy, Carothers Edmonds asserts his superiority over his Negro foster-brother and then, seeking later to repent, finds the tie irrevocably broken and his foster-family, though wonderfully cordial, stonily implacable; and the failure of love which Edmonds's tradition imposed upon him seems to affect his whole life.

## ISAAC MCCASLIN'S ROMANTICISM

As against the tradition which arrests the dignity of possession and the family, Isaac McCaslin sets the dignity of freedom and the unpossessable wilderness. The experience by which his moral sensibility is developed is a kind of compendium of the best American romantic and transcendental feeling. Cooper, Thoreau, and Melville are all comprised in what he learns from Sam Fathers, the Chickasaw Indian (but he was enough of a Negro to be glad to die), from the humility and discipline of hunting, from the quest after the great bear, a kind of forest cousin to Moby Dick, from the mysterious wilderness itself. So taught, he can no longer continue in the tradition to which he is born; at great and lasting cost to himself he surrenders his ancestral farm to the Edmonds branch.

It will of course be obvious that so personal and romantic a resolution as Ike McCaslin's is not being offered by Mr. Faulkner as a 'solution' to the racial problem of the South; nor, in representing that problem through the sexual and blood relations of Negro and white, is he offering a comprehensive description of the problem in all its literalness. (Though here I should like to suggest that Mr. Faulkner may be hinting that the Southern problem, in so far as it is cultural, is to be found crystallized in its sexual attitudes: it is certainly worth remarking of this book that white women are singularly absent from it and are scarcely mentioned, that all the significant relations are between men, and that Isaac McCaslin is the only man who loves a woman.) But the romantic and transcendental resolution and the blood and sexual ties are useful fictional symbols to represent the urgency and the iniquity of the literal fact. They suggest that its depth and its complication go beyond what committees and commissions can conceive, beyond even the most liberal 'understanding' and the most humanitarian 'sympathy'. Mr. Faulkner not only states this in the course of his book; he himself provides the proof: the story 'Pantaloon in Black' is conceived in 'understanding' and 'sympathy', like every other lynching story we have ever read, and when it is set beside the McCaslin stories with their complicated insights it appears not only inadequate but merely formal, almost insincere.

# The Theme of Maturation in *Intruder in the Dust*

Walter Brylowski

Walter Brylowski maintains that in *Intruder in the Dust* Faulkner presents his theme with reason, not action as he usually does. After Negro Lucas Beauchamp pulls young, white Chick Mallison from icy water, Chick feels obligated to repay his rescuer, but Lucas refuses his offers. Gavin Stevens uses reason to help the young boy grow up: to understand his experiences and to relate them to his community. Walter Brylowski has taught English at Michigan State, the University of Connecticut, and Eastern Michigan University.

*Intruder in the Dust* presents us with a modern ethical initiation of a young boy [Chick Mallison]. The initiation is, however, far removed from the realm of myth and one must extend himself to speak of the "rites" involved. Andrew Lytle, in a review of the book, says that the point of view in the novel "rests at last not upon the boy's coming into manhood, but upon manhood, or its essence: The Man." Giving the novel the benefit of his own Southern heritage, Lytle says,

> The South's hope for regeneration lies in its struggle itself to restore, not from outside pressure, to that part of its population the rights of manhood of which it is deprived. Understanding of this is proof of the boy's initiation and his right to the toga virilis.[1]

For him, Lucas Beauchamp occupies the position of "basic symbol of the Southern predicament," and the boy's initiation is to be viewed in terms of "the boy's active identity with

1. a white toga symbolizing manhood worn by fifteen-year-old Roman boys

the basic symbol":

> At the opening of the book on a hunting trip to the plantation
> he falls into a creek of icy water, in November, goes under
> three times and comes up to confront Lucas: the first en-
> counter. The shock of the experience and the sight of Lucas
> immediately afterwards . . . is a kind of baptism from which he
> will forevermore be changed. Even the time of the year marks
> it, the dead season which always precedes regeneration.

This is as far as one can safely go in describing the action in
terms of ritual.

## Chick Acts to Repay Lucas

Compared to the story of Isaac McCaslin, *Intruder in the
Dust* again offers Faulkner's tendency to offer us one story
going "downward" and one story going "upward." In Isaac
McCaslin we had the young initiate whose knowledge of the
"mysteries" of his society led him to a repudiation and di-
vorcement from that society; in the story of Chick Mallison
we have the story of a young boy who learns of his society
but takes action within that society and does not repudiate it.
Chick, at the age of twelve, has fallen through the ice while
hunting. Lucas appears on the scene and herds Chick and
the two Negro boys who are with him to his own house
where his clothes are dried and he is fed. Mrs. Vickery has
observed that at this point Chick accepts, without thinking,
the differences between the white and black worlds; that
having been fed and sheltered, his attempt at payment is a
perversion of the host-guest relationship into that of a
Negro-white relationship. The money falls to the floor and
Lucas commands one of the Negro boys to pick it up and return it to Chick. After that he lives with the necessity of re-
deeming his social error and of freeing himself of his obligation to Lucas. He sends the gift of the dress to Molly, Lucas'
wife, but the gift is cancelled out when Lucas sends him the
gallon of molasses. Then three years later, he passes Lucas
on the street and Lucas makes no sign of recognition; and
Chick thinks,

> *He didn't even fail to remember me this time. He didn't even
> know me. He hasn't even bothered to forget me:* thinking in a
> sort of peace even: *It's over. That was all* because he was free,
> the man who for three years had obsessed his life waking and
> sleeping too had walked out of it.

But when Lucas is picked up for the murder of a white
man and a lynching seems inevitable, Chick knows he has

not been free, that Lucas' hospitality has bound him in something more than a social obligation. His first impulse is to saddle his horse and ride out of town, ride so far that by the time he returns it will be all over. But where Isaac had sacrificed the land to gain his peace, Chick knows that it is irresponsibility that he must sacrifice to gain *his* peace and he does not ride away but instead goes to the graveyard with Miss Habersham and Aleck Sander to dig up the corpse, an action that proves Lucas' innocence.

## CHICK LEARNS THE MEANING OF HIS EXPERIENCE

The larger part of the novel, divorced from the frequent grave openings, is given over to the understanding Chick gains from his experience. Faulkner insists on the distinction between two kinds of knowledge or belief, that of rational empiricism which he repeatedly attributes to the world of men and that of simple intuition which he equally often attributes to women and children. While women and children may act wisely in terms of their special kind of knowledge, it is necessary, however, that this knowledge be translated into the realm of the rational-empiric if it is to be socially effective.

> The problem of the child emerging into manhood is, in a sense, a verbal one, for he is compelled to reconcile language with experience and in the light of their significant interaction to accept, reject, or redefine his tradition. In such a situation there is room not only for the revivifying action of Chick but for the verbal readjustments of Gavin Stevens.

The role of Gavin Stevens in the novel has been attacked primarily on the basis of his verbosity. Cleanth Brooks effectively refutes the position that Stevens should be regarded as Faulkner's spokesman:

> Doubtless, what he says often represents what many Southerners think and what Faulkner himself—at one time or another—has thought. But Gavin is not presented as the sage and wise counselor of the community. His notions have to take their chances along with those of less "intellectual" characters.

But while Stevens may be discarded as Faulkner's spokesman, it should be noted that the political views he expresses in this novel are quite similar to those Faulkner himself will reiterate in *Requiem for a Nun* where the prose sections attack the concept of a political order imposing social order upon the individual, relieving the individual of the necessity or right of formulating his own ethical principles.

Even if that social order is a desirable one, as an equality among the races is, it must be arrived at through an ethical judgment on the part of the individual, not legislated by the body politic. It is Gavin's role to orient Chick's knowledge based on experience to an effective social understanding.

> Gavin Stevens concerns himself with fostering Chick's intellectual comprehension of public morality and social relationships. Chick's venture into Beat Four to open a Gowrie grave, despite his knowledge that even his uncle would not understand or approve, constitutes his excursion into the wilderness. On his return, he, like Isaac, is ready to repudiate society and to isolate himself from it. Because of Stevens' efforts, he does not do so; he returns into history and time, a step that Isaac never took. In so doing he . . . establishes once more the identification of the individual's interests with those of the community even as he affirms the responsibility of the individual not only for his own conduct but for the conduct of all men.

## CHICK RECONCILES HIS EXPERIENCE WITH THE COMMUNITY

The greatest reconciliation Chick must make as a result of his experience is with the community as a whole. After the sheriff returns to town with the evidence that proves Lucas' innocence, Chick, through the car window, sees the face of the mob gathered to be present at the Gowries' vengeance:

> . . . not faces, but a face, not a mass nor even a mosaic of them but a Face: not even ravening nor uninsatiate but just in motion, insensate, vacant of thought or even passion: an Expression significantless and without past . . . without dignity and not even evocative horror: just neckless slack-muscled and asleep, hanging suspended face to face with him just beyond the glass of the back window.

As soon as the news spreads that Lucas is not guilty, the mob evaporates. Chick, giddy with sleeplessness, can hang on only to the fact that "They ran." This refrain recurs throughout his musings. The source of his contempt for the mob is that at this moment they made no gesture toward Lucas to absolve themselves of their guilt. It is Chick's disgust that Gavin Stevens must attempt to mitigate:

> ". . . there is a simple numerical point [Stevens tells him] at which a mob cancels and abolishes itself, maybe because it has finally got too big for darkness, the cave it was spawned in is no longer big enough to conceal it from light and so at last whether it will or not it has to look at itself. . . . Or maybe it's because man having passed into mob passes then into mass which abolishes mob by absorption, metabolism, then having got too large even for mass becomes man again con-

ceptible of pity and justice and conscience even if only in the recollection of his long painful aspiration toward them, toward that something anyway of one serene universal light."

"So man is always right," he [Chick] said.

"No," his uncle said. "He tries to be if they who use him for their own power and aggrandisement let him alone. Pity and justice and conscience too—that belief in more than the divinity of individual man . . . but in the divinity of his continuity as Man."

This theme will become central in *A Fable* where Faulkner offers the apotheosis[2] of his transcendental vision. Here we find Faulkner reaching back behind the crystallized forces of law to the spirit of the community. . . .

This searching for the relationship of the individual to the forms of society and the transcendence of these forms to once again recreate the community of man, to discover "the divinity of his continuity," is central to Faulkner's writing.

*Intruder in the Dust* constitutes one of Faulkner's unusual experiments in that here his vision is presented largely in the rational-empiric mode. The entire meaning of Chick's experience is handled in terms of a rational consideration. Faulkner does not employ his usual technique of presenting this resolution and reconciliation through action.

---

2. a person or thing exalted to godlike rank

# CHRONOLOGY

**1897**

William Faulkner born September 25

**1898**

Family moves to Ripley, Mississippi; Ernest Hemingway born; Steven Benet born

**1899**

Brother Murry C. (Jack) Falkner Jr. born

**1901**

Brother John Wesley Thompson (Johncy) Falkner III born; first transatlantic radio (wireless) transmission; Theodore Roosevelt becomes president (1901–1909)

**1902**

Family moves to Oxford, Mississippi

**1903**

Wright brothers invent the airplane

**1905**

Enters first grade, Oxford Grade School

**1906**

Skips to third grade; grandmother Sallie Murry Falkner dies

**1907**

Grandmother Lelia Dean Swift Butler dies; brother Dean Swift Falkner born; Model T Ford first mass-produced

**1909**

Works in father's livery stables; Howard Taft becomes president (1909–1913)

**1911**

Develops friendship with Estelle Oldham

**1913**

Woodrow Wilson becomes president (1913–1921)

**1914**

Beginning of friendship with Phil Stone; drops out of Oxford High School; World War I begins in Europe; Panama Canal opens

**1915**

Bear hunting at Phil Stone's family camp

**1916**

Works as bank clerk

**1917**

United States enters World War I

**1918**

Joins RAF Toronto, Canada; Estelle Oldham marries Cornell Franklin

**1919**

Travels around South; poem published in the *New Republic;* enters University of Mississippi as special admission; Treaty of Versailles

**1920**

Wins ten dollars in poetry contest; withdraws from the university; writes six copies of the play *The Marionettes,* by hand; sells five copies; first commercial radio broadcast

**1921**

Gives Estelle Franklin *Vision of Spring,* a volume of poems; works as bookstore clerk; becomes postmaster at university post office; Andrew Harding becomes president (1921–1923)

**1922**

Becomes Boy Scout leader; poem published in New Orleans *Double Dealer;* grandfather J.W.T. Falkner II dies

**1923**

Calvin Coolidge becomes president (1923–1929)

**1924**

*The Marble Faun* published; removed as scout leader because of drinking; resigns as postmaster after charges brought by postal inspector

**1925**

Contributes to New Orleans *Times Picayune*; travels to Europe; Scopes trial

**1926**

*Soldiers' Pay* published; writes *Helen: A Courtship*, a handwritten book of poems for Helen Baird; Byrd flies over North Pole

**1927**

*Mosquitoes* published; Lindbergh flight, New York to Paris

**1929**

*Sartoris* published; *The Sound and the Fury* published; marries Estelle Franklin; takes job at power plant; Herbert Hoover becomes president (1929–1933); stock market crash marks beginning of Great Depression

**1930**

*As I Lay Dying* published; purchases Rowan Oak

**1931**

*Sanctuary* published; *These 13* published; daughter Alabama born; lives nine days

**1932**

*Light in August* published; first MGM contract; father dies; Charles Lindbergh Jr. kidnapped and murdered

**1933**

*A Green Bough* published; daughter Jill born; begins flying lessons; Franklin D. Roosevelt becomes president (1933–1945)

**1934**

*Doctor Martino and Other Stories* published

**1935**

*Pylon* published; meets Meta Carpenter; Works Progress Administration and Social Security programs established

**1936**

*Absalom, Absalom!* published

**1938**

*The Unvanquished* published; MGM buys screen rights; buys Greenfield Farm

**1939**

*The Wild Palms* published; elected to National Institute of Arts and Letters; World War II begins in Europe

**1940**

*The Hamlet* published; Mammy Callie dies

**1941**

Japanese attack Pearl Harbor; United States enters World War II

**1942**

*Go Down, Moses* published

**1945**

Harry Truman becomes president (1945–1953); atomic bombs dropped on Hiroshima and Nagasaki; end of World War II

**1946**

*The Portable Faulkner*, edited by Malcolm Cowley, published; first meeting of the United Nations

**1947**

Meets with six classes at University of Mississippi, the first of his teaching-lecturing appearances; Marshall Plan for postwar reconstruction

**1948**

*Intruder in the Dust* published; MGM buys screen rights; elected to American Academy of Arts and Letters; Berlin blockade and airlift

**1949**

*Knight's Gambit* published; *Intruder in the Dust* filmed in Oxford

**1950**

*Collected Stories of William Faulkner* published; receives Howells Medal for fiction; receives Nobel Prize for literature; Korean War begins

**1951**

*Notes on a Horsethief* published; *Requiem for a Nun* published and staged; received National Book Award for *Collected Stories*; receives French Legion of Honor

**1953**

Dwight Eisenhower becomes president (1953–1961); truce in Korea

**1954**

*A Fable* published; attends São Paulo International Writers' Conference; Jill marries Paul D. Summers Jr.

**1955**

*Big Woods* published; receives National Book Award for fiction for *A Fable;* wins Pulitzer Prize for *A Fable;* lectures at University of Oregon and Montana State University; travels to Japan for State Department; Supreme Court orders school desegregation

**1956**

Becomes chairman of Writers' Group, People-to-People Program; grandson Paul D. Summers III born

**1957**

*The Town* published; writer-in-residence at University of Virginia; travels to Athens for State Department; receives Silver Medal of Greek Academy; National Guard sent to Little Rock, Arkansas, in school integration crisis

**1958**

Returns as writer-in-residence at University of Virginia; grandson William Cuthbert Falkner Summers born; Alaska admitted as forty-ninth state; United States launches first satellite

**1959**

*The Mansion* published; purchases home in Charlottesville, Virginia; Hawaii admitted as fiftieth state

**1960**

Appointed to faculty at University of Virginia

**1961**

Travels to Venezuela for State Department; grandson A. Burks Summers born; John F. Kennedy becomes president (1961–1963)

**1962**

*The Reivers* published; receives Gold Medal for fiction from the National Institutes of Arts and Letters; injured in fall from horse in Oxford; dies of heart attack on July 7; buried in St. Peter's Cemetery, Oxford

# FOR FURTHER RESEARCH

## ABOUT WILLIAM FAULKNER AND HIS WORKS

Ann Abadie, ed., *William Faulkner: A Life on Paper.* Jackson: University Press of Mississippi, 1980. (A transcription of the film produced by the Mississippi Center for Educational Television)

Walter Allen, *The Modern Novel in Britain and United States.* New York: E.P. Dutton, 1964.

Joseph Blotner, *Faulkner: A Biography.* New York: Random House, 1984.

Louis Daniel Brodsky, *William Faulkner, Life Glimpses.* Austin: University of Texas Press, 1990.

Jack Cofield, *William Faulkner: The Cofield Collection.* Oxford, MS: Yoknapatawpha Press, 1978.

Peter Conn, *Literature in America: An Illustrated History.* New York: Cambridge University Press, 1989.

Malcolm Cowley, *The Faulkner-Cowley File: Letters and Memories, 1944–1962.* New York: Penguin Books, 1966.

——, *The Flower and the Leaf: A Contemporary Record of American Writing Since 1941.* New York: Viking Penguin, 1985.

Marshall B. Davidson, *The American Heritage History of the Writers' America.* New York: American Heritage, 1960.

John Gardner, *On Writers and Writing.* Reading, MA: Addison-Wesley, 1994.

Maxwell Geismer, *Writers in Crises: The American Novel, 1925–1940.* Boston: Houghton Mifflin, 1942.

Albert J. Guerard, *The Triumph of the Novel: Dickens, Dostoevsky, Faulkner.* New York: Oxford University Press, 1976.

Oakley Hall, *The Art and Craft of Novel Writing.* Cincinnati: Writer's Digest Books, 1989.

Daniel Hoffman, *Faulkner's Country Matters.* Baton Rouge: Louisiana State University Press, 1989.

Frederick J. Hoffman, *The Modern Novel in America.* Chicago: Henry Regnery, 1951.

——, *William Faulkner.* New York: Twayne, 1961.

Frederick J. Hoffman and Olga W. Vickery, eds., *William Faulkner: Two Decades of Criticism.* East Lansing: Michigan State College Press, 1951.

James B. Meriwether and Michael Millgate, *Lion in the Garden: Interviews with William Faulkner 1926–1962.* New York: Random House, 1968.

Arthur Mezener, *The Sense of Life in the Modern Novel.* Boston: Houghton Mifflin, 1963.

Michael Millgate, *The Achievement of William Faulkner.* Lincoln: University of Nebraska Press, 1963.

Michael Millgate, ed., *New Essays on* Light in August. New York: Cambridge University Press, 1987.

Stephen B. Oates, *William Faulkner: The Man and the Artist: A Biography.* New York: Harper & Row, 1987.

William Van O'Connor, ed., *Seven Modern American Novelists: An Introduction.* Minneapolis: University of Minnesota Press, 1959.

Willard Thorp, *American Writing in the Twentieth Century.* Cambridge, MA: Harvard University Press, 1960.

## ABOUT FAULKNER'S TIME AND REGION

Hodding Carter, *Southern Legacy.* Baton Rouge: Louisiana State University Press, 1966.

W.J. Cash, *The Mind of the South.* New York: Vintage Books, 1941.

Thomas D. Clark, *The Emerging South.* 2nd ed. New York: Oxford University Press, 1968.

J. Richard Cohen and Steve Fiffer, eds., *Free at Last: A History of the Civil Rights Movement and Those Who Died in the Struggle.* Montgomery, AL: Southern Poverty Law Center, n.d.

The Editors of Time-Life Books, *Hard Times: 1930–1940.* This Fabulous Century Series. Alexandria, VA: Time-Life Books, 1969.

John Kenneth Galbraith, *The Great Crash 1929.* Boston: Houghton Mifflin, 1954.

Robert Goldston, *The Great Depression: The United States in the Thirties.* New York: Bobbs-Merrill, 1968.

Dewey W. Grantham, *The South in Modern America: A Region at Odds.* New York: HarperCollins, 1994.

Joe H. Kirchberger, *The Civil War and Reconstruction: An Eyewitness History.* New York: Facts On File, 1991.

Katherine Du Pre Lumpkin, *The Making of a Southerner.* New York: Knopf, 1947.

Ralph McGill, *The South and the Southerner.* Boston: Little, Brown, 1964.

Milton Meltzer, ed., *The American Promise: Voices of a Changing Nation, 1945–Present.* New York: Bantam Books, 1990.

Douglas T. Miller and Marion Nowak, *The Fifties: The Way We Really Were.* Garden City, NY: Doubleday, 1977.

John Osborne, ed., *The Old South: Alabama, Florida, Georgia, Mississippi, South Carolina.* New York: Time-Life Books, 1968.

Arnold Rose, *The Negro in America.* Boston: Beacon Press, 1956.

Herman E. Taylor, *Faulkner's Oxford: Recollections and Reflections.* Nashville, TN: Rutledge Hill Press, 1990.

Twelve Southerners, *I'll Take My Stand: The South and the Agrarian Tradition.* Introduction by Louis D. Rubin Jr. New York: Harper & Brothers, 1962.

Robert Weisbrot, *Marching Toward Freedom: 1957–1965.* New York: Chelsea House, 1994.

C. Vann Woodward, *The Strange Career of Jim Crow.* Rev. ed. New York: Oxford University Press, 1957.

# Works by William Faulkner

*The Marble Faun* (1924)

*Soldiers' Pay* (1926)

*Mosquitoes* (1927)

*Sartoris* (1929)

*The Sound and the Fury* (1929)

*As I Lay Dying* (1930)

*Sanctuary* (1931)

*Light in August* (1932)

*A Green Bough* (1933)

*Doctor Martino and Other Stories* (1934)

*Pylon* (1935)

*Absalom, Absalom!* (1936)

*The Unvanquished* (1938)

*The Wild Palms* (1939)

*The Hamlet* (1940)

*Go Down, Moses* (1942)

*The Portable Faulkner*, edited by Malcolm Cowley (1946)

*Intruder in the Dust* (1948)

*Knight's Gambit* (1949)

*Collected Stories of William Faulkner* (1950)

*Notes on a Horsethief* (1951)

*Requiem for a Nun* (1951)

*A Fable* (1954)

*Big Woods* (1955)

*The Town* (1957)

*The Mansion* (1959)

*The Reivers* (1962)

# INDEX